Private
Oral Exam Guide
by Michael D. Hayes

Eighth Edition

The comprehensive
guide to prepare you
for the FAA Oral Exam

Aviation Supplies & Academics, Inc.
Newcastle, Washington

Private Oral Exam Guide
Eighth Edition

Aviation Supplies & Academics, Inc.
7005 132nd Place SE
Newcastle, Washington 98059-3153

Visit the ASA website often (**www.asa2fly.com**, Product Updates link)
to find updates posted there due to FAA revisions to regulations that
may affect this book.

© 1992–2005 Aviation Supplies & Academics, Inc. All rights reserved.
Eighth Edition published 2005.

Printed in the United States of America

11   10   09   08   9   8   7   6   5   4

ASA-OEG-P8
ISBN 1-56027-579-0
      978-1-56027-579-4

Library of Congress Cataloging-in-Publication Data:

Hayes, Michael D.
   Private oral exam guide: the comprehensive guide to prepare
   you for the FAA Oral exam / by Michael D. Hayes.
         p.   cm.
      "ASA-OEG-P"—Cover.
   1. Aeronautics—Examinations, questions, etc. 2. Private
   flying—Examinations, questions, etc. 3. United States. Federal
   Aviation Administration—Examinations—Study guides.
   4. Oral examinations. I. Aviation Supplies & Academics, Inc.
   II. Title.
   TL546.5.H33   1993
   629.132'5217'076—dc20   93-12050
                                              CIP

This guide is dedicated to the many talented students, pilots and flight instructors I have had the opportunity to work with over the years. Also, special thanks to Mark Hayes and many others who supplied the patience, encouragement, and understanding necessary to complete the project.

—M.D.H.

Contents

Introduction

The *Private Oral Exam Guide* is a comprehensive guide designed for student pilots who are involved in training for the Private Pilot Certificate. This guide was originally designed for use in a 14 CFR Part 141 flight school but has quickly become popular with those training under Part 61 and are not affiliated with an FAA-approved school. The guide will also prove beneficial to private pilots who wish to refresh their knowledge or who are preparing for a flight review.

The Private Pilot Practical Test Standards book (FAA-S-8081-14A) specifies the areas in which knowledge must be demonstrated by the applicant before issuance of a pilot certificate or rating. The *Private Oral Exam Guide* has been designed to evaluate a pilot's knowledge of those areas. This guide contains questions and answers organized into eight main divisions which represent those areas of knowledge required for the practical test.

At any time during the practical test, an FAA examiner may ask questions pertaining to any of the subject areas within these divisions. Through very intensive post-private pilot checkride debriefings, we have provided you with the most consistent questions asked along with the information necessary for a knowledgeable response. The guide may be supplemented with other comprehensive study

Continued

materials as noted in parentheses after each question. For example: (FAA-H-8083-3). The abbreviations for these materials and their titles are listed below. Be sure to use the latest revision of these references when reviewing for the test.

14 CFR Part 1	*Definitions and Abbreviations*
14 CFR Part 43	*Maintenance, Preventive Maintenance, Rebuilding, and Alteration*
14 CFR Part 61	*Certification: Pilots, Flight Instructors, and Ground Instructors*
14 CFR Part 91	*General Operating and Flight Rules*
NTSB Part 830	*Notification and Reporting of Aircraft Accidents and Incidents*
AC 00-6	*Aviation Weather*
AC 00-45	*Aviation Weather Services*
AC 61-67	*Stall and Spin Awareness Training*
AC 91-67	*Minimum Equipment Requirements for General Aviation Operations Under FAR Part 91*
FAA-H-8081-14	*Private Pilot Practical Test Standards*
FAA-H-8083-1	*Aircraft Weight & Balance Handbook*
FAA-H-8083-3	*Airplane Flying Handbook*
FAA-H-8083-9	*Aviation Instructor's Handbook*
FAA-H-8083-15	*Instrument Flying Handbook*
FAA-H-8083-25	*Pilot's Handbook of Aeronautical Knowledge*
FAA-P-8740-2	*Density Altitude*
FSAT 00-09	*Increased Surveillance and Testing of Surface Movement Operations*
AIM	*Aeronautical Information Manual*
POH	*Pilot Operating Handbook*
AFM	*FAA-Approved Airplane Flight Manual*
NACO	National Aeronautical Charting Office

Most of the publications listed above are reprinted by ASA and are available from aviation retailers nationwide.

A review of the information presented within this guide should provide the necessary preparation for the FAA Private Pilot Certification Practical test.

Certificates
and Documents

1

A. Certification

What are the eligibility requirements for a private pilot (airplane) certificate? (14 CFR 61.103)

a. Be at least 17 years of age.

b. Be able to read, speak, write, and understand the English language.

c. Hold at least a current Third Class medical certificate.

d. Received the required ground and flight training endorsements.

e. Meet the applicable aeronautical experience requirements.

f. Passed the required knowledge and practical tests.

B. Privileges and Limitations

1. What privileges and limitations apply to a private pilot? (14 CFR 61.113)

No person who holds a private pilot certificate may act as a pilot-in-command of an aircraft that is carrying passengers or property for compensation or hire; nor may that person, for compensation or hire, act as pilot-in-command of an aircraft. A private pilot—

a. may act as PIC of an aircraft in connection with any business or employment if it is only incidental to that business or employment and does not carry passengers or property for compensation or hire.

b. may not pay less than the pro rata share of the operating expenses of a flight with passengers, provided the expenses involve only fuel, oil, airport expenditures, or rental fees.

c. may act as PIC of an aircraft used in a passenger-carrying airlift sponsored by certain charitable organizations.

d. may be reimbursed for aircraft operating expenses that are directly related to search and location operations, provided the expenses involve only fuel, oil, airport expenditures, or rental fees, and the operation is sanctioned and under the direction and control of local, state or federal agencies or organizations that conduct search and location operations.

Continued

    e. may demonstrate an aircraft in flight to a prospective buyer if the private pilot is an aircraft salesman and has at least 200 hours of logged flight time.

    f. may act as PIC of an aircraft towing a glider provided they meet the requirements of 14 CFR 61.69.

2. To act as pilot-in-command, or in any other capacity as a required flight crewmember of a civil aircraft, what must a pilot have in his/her physical possession or readily accessible in the aircraft? (14 CFR 61.3)

    a. A valid pilot certificate

    b. A photo identification

    c. A current and appropriate medical certificate.

3. What is the definition of a high-performance airplane, and what must you do to act as pilot-in-command of such an airplane? (14 CFR 61.31)

A high-performance airplane is an airplane with an engine of more than 200 horsepower. To act as PIC of a high-performance airplane you must have:

    a. received and logged ground and flight training from an authorized flight instructor in a high-performance airplane, or in a flight simulator or flight training device that is representative of a high-performance airplane and have been found proficient in the operation and systems of that airplane.

    b. received and logged a one-time endorsement in your logbook from an authorized instructor who certifies you are proficient to operate a high-performance airplane.

Note: The training and endorsement required by this regulation is not required if the person has logged flight time as PIC of a high-performance airplane, or in a flight simulator or flight training device that is representative of a high-performance airplane prior to August 4, 1997.

4. Other than high-performance and complex aircraft, what other types of aircraft (ASEL) require specific training and logbook endorsements from an appropriately rated flight instructor? (14 CFR 61.31)

High-Altitude Airplane — No person may act as pilot-in-command of a pressurized airplane that has a service ceiling or maximum operating altitude (whichever is lower), above 25,000 feet MSL unless that person has completed the ground and flight training specified and has received a logbook or training record endorsement from an authorized instructor certifying satisfactory completion of the training.

Tailwheel Airplane — No person may act as pilot-in-command of a tailwheel airplane unless that pilot has received flight instruction from an authorized flight instructor who has found the pilot competent to operate a tailwheel airplane and has made a one-time endorsement so stating in the pilot's logbook. The endorsement is not required if a pilot has logged flight time as pilot-in-command of tailwheel airplanes prior to April 15, 1991.

5. What is the definition of a complex airplane, and what must you do to act as pilot-in-command of such an airplane? (14 CFR 61.31)

A complex airplane is an airplane that has a retractable landing gear, flaps, and a controllable pitch propeller. You must have:

a. received and logged ground and flight training from an authorized flight instructor in a complex airplane, or in a flight simulator or flight training device that is representative of a complex airplane and have been found proficient in the operation and systems of that airplane.

b. received a one-time endorsement in your logbook from an authorized instructor who certifies you are proficient to operate a complex airplane.

Note: The training and endorsement required by this regulation is not required if the person has logged flight time as PIC of a complex airplane, or in a flight simulator or flight training device that is representative of a complex airplane prior to August 4, 1997.

6. **With respect to certification, privileges, and limitations of airmen, define the terms: "Category," "Class," and "Type."** (14 CFR Part 1)

Category—a broad classification of aircraft; i.e., airplane, rotorcraft, glider, etc.

Class—a classification of aircraft within a category having similar operating characteristics; i.e., single-engine land, multi-engine land, etc.

Type—a specific make and basic model of aircraft including modifications that do not change its handling or flight characteristics; i.e., DC-9, B-737, C-150, etc.

C. Currency Requirements

1. **What are the requirements to remain current as a private pilot?** (14 CFR 61.56, 61.57)

   a. Within the preceding 24 months, accomplished a flight review given in an aircraft for which that pilot is rated by an authorized instructor and received a logbook endorsement certifying that the person has satisfactorily completed the review.

   b. To carry passengers, a pilot must have made, within the preceding 90 days—

      • three takeoffs and landings as the sole manipulator of flight controls of an aircraft of the same category and class and, if a type rating is required, of the same type.

      • if the aircraft is a tailwheel airplane, the landings must have been made to a full stop in an airplane with a tailwheel.

      • if operations are to be conducted during the period beginning 1 hour after sunset and ending 1 hour before sunrise, with passengers on board, the PIC must have, within the preceding 90 days, made at least three takeoffs and three landings to a full stop during that period in an aircraft of the same category, class, and type (if a type is required) of aircraft to be used.

   Note: Takeoffs and landings required by this regulation may be accomplished in a flight simulator or flight training device that is approved by the Administrator and used in accordance with an approved course conducted by a certificated training center.

2. **To exercise the privileges of a private pilot certificate, what medical certificate is required, and how long is it valid?** (14 CFR 61.23)

You must possess a third-class medical certificate. If the medical certificate was issued before September 16, 1996, it expires at the end of the 24th month after the month of the date of examination shown on the certificate. If it was issued on or after September 16, 1996, it expires at the end of:

a. The 36th month after the month of the date of the examination shown on the certificate if the person has not reached his or her 40th birthday on or before the date of examination; or

b. The 24th month after the month of the date of the examination shown on the certificate if the person has reached his or her 40th birthday on or before the date of the examination.

3. **If a pilot changes his/her permanent mailing address and fails to notify the FAA Airmen Certification branch of the new address, how long may the pilot continue to exercise the privileges of his/her pilot certificate?** (14 CFR 61.60)

30 days after the date of the move.

D. Aircraft Certificates and Documents

1. **What documents are required on board an aircraft prior to flight?** (14 CFR 91.203, 91.9)

A irworthiness Certificate
R egistration Certificate
O wner's manual or operating limitations
W eight and balance data

2. **How can a pilot determine if his/her aircraft is equipped with a Mode C altitude encoding transponder?**

By referencing the current weight and balance equipment list for that aircraft, a pilot could positively determine whether or not a Mode C transponder is installed.

3. When will an aircraft registration certificate expire? (FAA-H-8083-25)

When any of the following occur:

a. The aircraft is registered under the laws of a foreign country.

b. The registration of the aircraft is canceled at the written request of the holder of the certificate.

c. The aircraft is totally destroyed or scrapped.

d. The ownership of the aircraft is transferred.

e. The holder of the certificate loses United States citizenship.

f. Thirty days have elapsed since the death of the holder of the certificate.

E. Aircraft Maintenance Requirements

1. Who is responsible for ensuring that an aircraft is maintained in an airworthy condition? (14 CFR 91.403)

The owner or operator of an aircraft is primarily responsible for maintaining an aircraft in an airworthy condition.

2. After aircraft inspections have been made and defects have been repaired, who is responsible for determining that the aircraft is in an airworthy condition? (14 CFR 91.7)

The pilot-in-command of a civil aircraft is responsible for determining whether that aircraft is in condition for safe flight. The pilot-in-command shall discontinue the flight when unairworthy mechanical, electrical, or structural conditions occur.

3. What records or documents should be checked to determine that the owner or operator of an aircraft has complied with all required inspections and airworthiness directives? (14 CFR 91.405)

The maintenance records (aircraft and engine logbooks). Each owner or operator of an aircraft shall ensure that maintenance personnel make appropriate entries in the aircraft maintenance records indicating the aircraft has been approved for return to service.

4. What regulations apply concerning the operation of an aircraft that has had alterations or repairs which may have substantially affected its operation in flight? (14 CFR 91.407)

No person may operate or carry passengers in any aircraft that has undergone maintenance, preventative maintenance, rebuilding, or alteration that may have appreciably changed its flight characteristics or substantially affected its operation in flight until an appropriately rated pilot with at least a private pilot certificate

a. flies the aircraft;

b. makes an operational check of the maintenance performed or alteration made; and

c. logs the flight in the aircraft records.

5. What is an Airworthiness Certificate and how long does it remain valid? (FAA-H-8083-25)

An Airworthiness Certificate is issued by the FAA only after the aircraft has been inspected and found to meet the requirements of 14 CFR, and is in a condition for safe operation. Under any circumstances, the aircraft must meet the requirements of the original type certificate. The certificate must be displayed in the aircraft so that it is legible to passengers or crew whenever the aircraft is operated, and it may be transferred with the aircraft except when sold to a foreign purchaser. Standard Airworthiness Certificates remain in effect as long as the aircraft receives the required maintenance and is properly registered in the United States.

6. Can a pilot conduct flight operations in an aircraft with known inoperative equipment? (AC 91-67, 14 CFR 91.213)

Yes, under specific conditions. 14 CFR Part 91 describes acceptable methods for the operation of an aircraft with certain inoperative instruments and equipment that are not essential for safe flight—they are:

a. Operation of aircraft with a Minimum Equipment List (MEL), as authorized by 14 CFR 91.213(a)

b. Operation of aircraft without a MEL under 14 CFR 91.213(d)

7. What are Minimum Equipment Lists? (AC 91-67)

The Minimum Equipment List (MEL) is a precise listing of instruments, equipment and procedures that allows an aircraft to be operated under specific conditions with inoperative equipment. The MEL is the specific inoperative equipment document for a particular make and model aircraft by serial and registration numbers; e.g., BE-200, N12345. The FAA-approved MEL includes only those items of equipment that the FAA deems may be inoperative and still maintain an acceptable level of safety with appropriate conditions and limitations.

8. What limitations apply to aircraft operations conducted using the deferral provision of 14 CFR 91.213(d)? (FAA-H-8083-25)

When inoperative equipment is found during preflight or prior to departure, the decision should be to cancel the flight, obtain maintenance prior to flight, or to defer the item or equipment. Maintenance deferrals are not used for inflight discrepancies. The manufacturer's AFM/POH procedures are to be used in those situations.

9. What limitations apply to aircraft operations being conducted using MELs? (FAA-H-8083-25)

The use of an MEL for a small, non-turbine-powered airplane operated under Part 91 allows for the deferral of inoperative items or equipment. The FAA considers an approved MEL to be a supplemental type certificate (STC) issued to an aircraft by serial number and registration number. Once an operator requests an MEL, and a Letter of Authorization (LOA) is issued by the FAA, then the MEL becomes mandatory for that airplane. All maintenance deferrals must be done in accordance with the MEL and the operator-generated procedures document.

10. What are the procedures to follow when using 14 CFR 91.213(d) for deferral of inoperative equipment? (FAA-H-8083-25)

The pilot determines whether the inoperative equipment is required by type design, the regulations, or ADs. If the inoperative item is not required, and the airplane can be safely operated without it, the deferral may be made. Then the pilot removes or deactivates the inoperative item, and places an INOPERATIVE placard near the appropriate switch, control, or indicator.

If deactivation or removal involves maintenance (removal always will), it must be accomplished by certificated maintenance personnel. For example, if the position lights (installed equipment) were discovered to be inoperative prior to a daytime flight, the pilot would follow the requirements of section 91.213(d).

11. What are the required maintenance inspections for aircraft? (14 CFR 91.409)

a. *Annual inspection*—within the preceding 12 calendar months

b. *100-hour inspection*—if carrying any person (other than a crewmember) for hire or giving flight instruction for hire.

If an aircraft is operated for hire it must have a 100-hour inspection as well as an annual inspection when due. If not operated for hire, it must have an annual inspection only.

12. If an aircraft has been on a schedule of inspection every 100 hours, under what condition may it continue to operate beyond the 100 hours without a new inspection? (14 CFR 91.409)

The 100-hour limitation may be exceeded by not more than 10 hours while en route to a place where the inspection can be done. The excess time used to reach a place where the inspection can be done must be included in computing the next 100 hours of time in service.

13. What is the difference between an annual inspection and a 100-hour inspection? (14 CFR Part 43)

No differences exist when comparing the content of an annual inspection with that of a 100-hour inspection. The difference is who is allowed to perform these inspections. Only an A&P mechanic with an Inspection Authorization can perform an annual inspection. 100-hour inspections may be performed by any A&P mechanic (no IA required).

14. Be capable of locating the required maintenance and equipment inspections for your aircraft in the aircraft and engine logbooks. What should these include? (14 CFR 91.207, 91.215, 91.405, and 91.413)

a. Annual inspection/100 hour inspection

b. ELT inspection (12 calendar months)

c. ELT battery expiration date

d. Transponder certification (24 calendar months)

e. Compliance with applicable ADs

Note: If operating under IFR, the pitot-static pressure system, altimeter, and automatic pressure altitude reporting system must also have been tested and inspected in the preceding 24 calendar months.

15. What are some of the responsibilities an aircraft owner has pertaining to aircraft documents, maintenance and inspections of their aircraft? (FAA-H-8083-25)

Aircraft owners must:

a. Have a current Airworthiness Certificate and Aircraft Registration in the aircraft.

b. Maintain the aircraft in an airworthy condition including compliance with all applicable Airworthiness Directives.

c. Ensure maintenance is properly recorded.

d. Keep abreast of current regulations concerning the operation of that aircraft.

e. Notify the FAA Civil Aviation Registry immediately of any change of permanent mailing address, or of the sale or export of the aircraft, or of the loss of citizenship.

f. Have a current FCC radio station license if equipped with radios, including emergency locator transmitter (ELT), if operated outside of the United States.

16. Define "preventive maintenance." (FAA-H-8083-25)

"Preventive maintenance" means simple or minor preservation operations and the replacement of small standard parts not involving complex assembly operations. Certificated pilots, excluding student pilots, sport pilots, and recreational pilots, may perform preventive maintenance on any aircraft that is owned or operated by them provided that aircraft is not used in air carrier service. 14 CFR Part 43 identifies typical preventive maintenance operations which include such basic items as oil changes, wheel bearing lubrication, hydraulic fluid (brakes, landing gear system) refills.

17. What are "Special Flight Permits," and when are they necessary? (14 CFR 91.213, 14 CFR 21.197)

A Special Flight Permit may be issued for an aircraft that may not currently meet applicable airworthiness requirements but is capable of safe flight. These permits are typically issued for the following purposes:

a. Flying an aircraft to a base where repairs, alterations or maintenance are to be performed, or to a point of storage.

b. Delivering or exporting an aircraft.

c. Production flight testing new-production aircraft.

d. Evacuating aircraft from areas of impending danger.

e. Conducting customer demonstration flights in new-production aircraft that have satisfactorily completed production flight tests.

18. How are "Special Flight Permits" obtained? (FAA-H-8083-25)

If a special flight permit is needed, assistance and the necessary forms may be obtained from the local FSDO or Designated Airworthiness Representative (DAR).

19. What are "Airworthiness Directives" (ADs)?
(FAA-H-8083-25)

An AD is the medium the FAA uses to notify aircraft owners and other potentially interested persons of unsafe conditions that may exist because of design defects, maintenance, or other causes, and to specify the conditions under which the product may continue to be operated. ADs are regulatory in nature, and compliance is mandatory. It is the aircraft owner's or operator's responsibility to ensure compliance with all pertinent ADs.

Additional Study Questions

1. As a newly certificated private pilot, you are ready to utilize your certificate. I am a friend and need you to fly a package to a distant destination. I will pay for the airplane if you accept. Do the regulations allow you to accept this offer? (14 CFR 61.113)

2. Is a Private Pilot required to log all flight time? (14 CFR 61.51)

3. If the aircraft has recently had a transfer of ownership, how long will the temporary registration certificate be valid? (14 CFR 47.31)

4. The regulations state that operating costs may be shared with your passengers. What percentage of the operating costs may be shared with the passengers? (14 CFR 61.113)

5. How can a pilot determine if all of the required placards are present in his/her airplane? (14 CFR Part 43)

6. Which documents, required on board an aircraft, must be displayed in such a way so as to be visible by both the passengers and crew? (14 CFR 91.203)

7. Preventive maintenance has been performed on an aircraft. What paperwork is required? (14 CFR 43.9)

8. How can a pilot determine if all applicable Airworthiness Directives have been complied with for his/her airplane? (14 CFR Part 43)

9. If the AFM for an aircraft you are about to fly is missing, what substitution may be made, if any? (14 CFR 91.9)

10. What is an "equipment list," and where is it normally located? (FAA-H-8083-1)

Weather 2

A. Nature of the Atmosphere

1. State the general characteristics in regard to the flow of air around high and low pressure systems in the Northern Hemisphere. (AC 00-6A)

Low Pressure—inward, upward, and counterclockwise
High Pressure—outward, downward, and clockwise

2. What is a "trough"? (AC 00-6A)

A trough (also called a trough line) is an elongated area of relatively low atmospheric pressure. At the surface when air converges into a low, it cannot go outward against the pressure gradient, nor can it go downward into the ground; it must go upward. Therefore, a low or trough is an area of rising air. Rising air is conducive to cloudiness and precipitation; hence the general association of low pressure and bad weather.

3. What is a "ridge"? (AC 00-6A)

A ridge (also called a ridge line) is an elongated area of relatively high atmospheric pressure. Air moving out of a high or ridge depletes the quantity of air; therefore, these are areas of descending air. Descending air favors dissipation of cloudiness; hence the association of high pressure and good weather.

4. What are the standard temperature and pressure values for sea level? (AC 00-6A)

15°C and 29.92" Hg

5. What are "isobars"? (AC 00-6A)

An isobar is a line on a weather chart which connects areas of equal or constant barometric pressure.

6. If the isobars are relatively close together on a surface weather chart or a constant pressure chart, what information will this provide? (AC 00-6A)

The spacing of isobars on these charts defines how steep or shallow a pressure gradient is. When isobars are spaced very close together, a steep pressure gradient exists which indicates higher wind speeds. A shallow pressure gradient (isobars not close together) usually means wind speeds will be less.

7. What causes the winds aloft to flow parallel to the isobars? (AC 00-6A)

The Coriolis force.

8. Why do surface winds generally flow across the isobars at an angle? (AC 00-6A)

Surface friction.

9. At what rate does atmospheric pressure decrease with an increase in altitude? (AC 00-6A)

1" Hg per 1,000 feet.

10. What does "dew point" mean? (AC 00-6A)

Dew point is the temperature to which a sample of air must be cooled to attain the state of saturation.

11. When temperature and dew point are close together (within 5°), what type of weather is likely? (AC 00-6A)

Visible moisture in the form of clouds, dew, or fog. Also, these are ideal conditions for carburetor icing.

12. What factor primarily determines the type and vertical extent of clouds? (AC 00-6A)

The stability of the atmosphere.

13. How do you determine the stability of the atmosphere? (AC 00-6A)

By observing the actual lapse rate and comparing it to the standard lapse rate of 3.5°F per 1,000 feet. The "K" index of a stability chart is the primary means of determining stability. In general, stable air cools at a rate less than the standard lapse rate with altitude, and unstable air cools at a rate that is greater than the standard lapse rate.

14. List the effects of stable and unstable air on clouds, turbulence, precipitation and visibility. (AC 00-6A)

	Stable	**Unstable**
Clouds	Stratiform	Cumuliform
Turbulence	Smooth	Rough
Precipitation	Steady	Showery
Visibility	Fair to Poor	Good

15. At what altitude above the surface would the pilot expect the bases of cumuliform clouds if the surface temperature is 82° and the dew point is 62°? (AC 00-6A)

You can estimate the height of cumuliform cloud bases using surface temperature/dewpoint spread. Unsaturated air in a convective current cools at about 5.4°F (3.0°C) per 1,000 feet; dew point decreases at about 1°F (5/9°C). Thus, in a convective current, temperature and dew point converge at about 4.4°F (2.5°C) per 1,000 feet. You can get a quick estimate of a convective cloud base in thousands of feet by rounding the values and dividing into the spread. When using Fahrenheit, divide by 4 and multiply by 1,000. This method of estimating is reliable only with instability, clouds and during the warmer part of the day.

$$\frac{\text{Temperature} - \text{dew point}}{4} \times 1,000 = \text{Base of clouds}$$

$82 - 62 = 20$

$20 \div 4 = 5$

$5 \times 1,000 = 5,000$ feet AGL

16. What will the freezing level be if the field elevation is 1,000 feet and the temperature at the surface is 15°C? (AC 00-6A)

The freezing level (0°C) can be estimated by subtracting 2°C per 1,000 feet (average lapse rate) from 15°C and then adding the result to the field elevation. For this example the freezing level will be at 8,500 MSL.

17. What conditions are necessary for structural icing to occur? (AC 00-6A)

Visible moisture and below freezing temperatures at the point moisture strikes the aircraft.

18. What are the two main types of icing? (AC 00-6A)

Structural and induction.

19. Name four types of structural ice. (AC 00-6A)

Clear ice—forms when large drops strike the aircraft surface and slowly freeze.

Rime ice—small drops strike the aircraft and freeze rapidly.

Mixed ice—combination of above; supercooled water drops varying in size.

Frost—ice crystal deposits formed by sublimation when temperature and dew point are below freezing.

20. What action is recommended if you inadvertently encounter icing conditions? (AC 00-6A)

Change course and/or altitude; usually, climb to a higher altitude, if possible.

21. Is frost considered to be hazardous to flight? Why? (AC 00-6A)

Yes, because while frost does not change the basic aerodynamic shape of the wing, the roughness of its surface spoils the smooth flow of air, thus causing a slowing of airflow. This slowing of the air causes early airflow separation, resulting in a loss of lift. Even a small amount of frost on airfoils may prevent an aircraft from becoming airborne at normal takeoff speed. It is also possible that, once airborne, an aircraft could have insufficient margin of airspeed above stall so that moderate gusts or turning flight could produce incipient or complete stalling.

22. What factors must be present for a thunderstorm to form? (AC 00-6A)

a. A source of lift (heating, fast-moving front)

b. Unstable air (nonstandard lapse rate)

c. High moisture content (temperature/dew point close)

23. What are the three stages of a thunderstorm? (AC 00-6A)

Cumulus stage—Updrafts cause raindrops to increase in size.

Mature stage—Rain at earth's surface; it falls through or immediately beside the updrafts; lightning; perhaps roll clouds.

Dissipating stage—Downdrafts and rain begin to dissipate.

24. What is a "temperature inversion"? (AC 00-6A)

An inversion is an increase in temperature with height—a reversal of the normal decrease with height. An inversion aloft permits warm rain to fall through cold air below. Temperature in the cold air can be critical to icing. A ground-based inversion favors poor visibility by trapping fog, smoke, and other restrictions into low levels of the atmosphere. The air is stable, with little or no turbulence.

25. State two basic ways that fog may form. (AC 00-6A)

a. Cool air to the dew point

b. Adding moisture to the air

26. Name several types of fog. (AC 00-6A)

a. Radiation fog

b. Advection fog

c. Upslope fog

d. Precipitation-induced fog

e. Ice fog

27. What causes radiation fog to form? (AC 00-6A)

The ground cools the adjacent air to the dew point on calm, clear nights.

28. What is advection fog, and where is it most likely to form? (AC 00-6A)

Advection fog results from the transport of warm humid air over a cold surface. A pilot can expect advection fog to form primarily along coastal areas during the winter. Unlike radiation fog, it may occur with winds, cloudy skies, over a wide geographic area, and at any time of the day or night.

29. What is upslope fog? (AC 00-6A)

Upslope fog forms as a result of moist, stable air being cooled adiabatically as it moves up sloping terrain. Once the upslope wind ceases, the fog dissipates. Upslope fog is often quite dense and extends to high altitudes.

30. Define the term "wind shear," and state the areas in which it is likely to occur. (AC 00-6A)

Wind shear is defined as the rate of change of wind velocity (direction and/or speed) per unit distance; conventionally expressed as vertical or horizontal wind shear. It may occur at any level in the atmosphere but three areas are of special concern:

a. Wind shear with a low-level temperature inversion.

b. Wind shear in a frontal zone or thunderstorm.

c. Clear air turbulence (CAT) at high levels associated with a jet stream or strong circulation.

31. Why is wind shear an operational concern to pilots? (AC 00-6A)

Wind shear is an operational concern because unexpected changes in wind speed and direction can be potentially very hazardous to aircraft operations at low altitudes on approach to and departing from airports.

B. Obtaining Weather Information

1. What is the primary means of obtaining a weather briefing? (AIM 7-1-2)

The primary source is an individual briefing obtained from a briefer at the AFSS/FSS. These briefings, which are tailored to your specific flight, are available 24 hours a day through the use of the toll-free number (1-800-WX BRIEF).

2. What are some examples of other sources of weather information? (AIM 7-1-2)

a. Telephone Information Briefing Service (TIBS) (AFSS)

b. Transcribed Weather Broadcasts (TWEB)

c. Telephone Access to TWEB (TEL-TWEB)

d. Weather and aeronautical information from numerous private industry sources

e. The Direct User Access System (DUATS)

3. Where can you find a listing of FSS and weather information numbers? (AIM 7-1-2)

Numbers for these services can be found in the Airport/Facility Directory under the "FAA and NWS Telephone Numbers" section. They are also listed in the U.S. Government section of the local telephone directory.

4. What types of weather briefings are available from an FSS briefer? (AIM 7-1-4)

Standard Briefing—Request when you are planning a flight and you have not received a previous briefing or have not received preliminary information through mass dissemination media (TIBS, TWEB, etc.).

Abbreviated Briefing—Request when you need information to supplement mass disseminated data, update a previous briefing, or when you need only one or two items.

Continued

Outlook Briefing—Request whenever your proposed time of departure is six or more hours from the time of the briefing; for planning purposes only.

Inflight Briefing—Request when needed to update a preflight briefing.

5. What pertinent information should a weather briefing include? (AIM 7-1-4)

a. Adverse Conditions

b. VFR Flight Not Recommended

c. Synopsis

d. Current Conditions

e. Enroute Forecast

f. Destination Forecast

g. Winds Aloft

h. Notices to Airmen (NOTAMs)

i. ATC Delay

j. Pilots may obtain the following from AFSS/FSS briefers upon request: Information on MTRs and MOAs, a review of printed NOTAM publications, approximate density altitude information, information on air traffic services and rules, customs/immigration procedures, ADIZ rules, search and rescue, LORAN, NOTAM, GPS RAIM availability, and other assistance as required.

6. What is EFAS? (AIM 7-1-5)

En route Flight Advisory Service (EFAS) is a service specifically designed to provide enroute aircraft with timely and meaningful weather advisories pertinent to the type of flight intended, route of flight, and altitude. In conjunction with this service, EFAS is also a central collection and distribution point for pilot reported weather information (PIREPs). EFAS provides communications capabilities for aircraft flying at 5,000 feet above ground level to 17,500 feet MSL on a common frequency of 122.0 MHz. It is also known as "Flight Watch."

7. What is HIWAS? (AIM 7-1-10)

Hazardous In-flight Weather Advisory Service (HIWAS) is a continuous broadcast of in-flight weather advisories including summarized Aviation Weather Warnings, SIGMETs, Convective SIGMETs, Center Weather Advisories, AIRMETs, and urgent PIREPs. HIWAS is an additional source of hazardous weather information which makes this data available on a continuous basis.

C. Aviation Weather Reports and Observations

1. What is a METAR? (AC 00-45E)

METAR, or Aviation Routine Weather Report: An hourly surface observation of conditions observed at an airport.

2. Describe the basic elements of a METAR. (AC 00-45E)

A METAR report contains the following elements in order as presented:

a. *Type of reports*—the METAR, and the SPECI (aviation special weather report).

b. *ICAO station identifier*—4-letter station identifiers; in the conterminous U.S., the 3-letter identifier is prefixed with K.

c. *Date and time of report*—a 6-digit date/time group appended with Z (UTC). First two digits are the date, then two for the hour, and two for minutes.

d. *Modifier (as required)*—if used, the modifier AUTO identifies the report as an automated weather report with no human intervention. If AUTO is shown in the body of the report, AO1 or AO2 will be encoded in the remarks section to indicate the type of precipitation sensor used at the station.

e. *Wind*—5-digit group (6 digits if speed is over 99 knots); first three digits = wind direction, in tens of degrees referenced to true north. Directions less than 100 degrees are preceded with a zero; next two digits are the average speed in knots, measured or estimated (or, if over 99 knots, the next three digits).

Continued

f. *Visibility: prevailing visibility*—statute miles, space, fractions of statute miles (as needed), and the letters SM.

g. *Runway visual range (RVR),* as required.

h. *Weather phenomena*—broken into two categories: qualifiers, and weather phenomena.

i. *Sky condition*—amount/height/type (as required) or indefinite ceiling/height (vertical visibility).

j. *Temperature/dew point group*—2-digit format in whole degrees Celsius, separated by a solidus (/). Temperatures below zero are prefixed with M.

k. *Altimeter*—4-digit format representing tens, units, tenths, and hundredths of inches of mercury prefixed with A. The decimal point is not reported or stated.

l. *Remarks (RMK), as required*—operational significant weather phenomena, location of phenomena, beginning and ending times, direction of movement.

Example: METAR KLAX 140651Z AUTO 00000KT 1SM
R35L/4500V6000FT -RA BR BKN030 10/10 A2990
RMK AO2

3. Describe several types of weather observing programs available. (AIM 7-1-12)

a. *Manual Observations*—reports made from airport locations staffed by FAA or NWS personnel.

b. *AWOS*—Automated Weather Observing System; consists of various sensors, a processor, a computer-generated voice sub-system, and a transmitter to broadcast local, minute-by-minute weather data directly to the pilot. Observations will include the prefix AUTO in data.

c. *AWOS Broadcasts*—computer-generated voice is used to auto-mate the broadcast of minute-by-minute weather observations.

d. *ASOS*—Automated Surface Observing System; the primary U.S. surface weather observing system. Up to 993 systems in-stalled throughout the U.S. providing minute-by-minute obser-vations generating METARs and other aviation weather information. Transmitted over a discrete VHF radio frequency or the voice portion of a local NAVAID. ASOS includes the prefix "AUTO" in the report data.

4. What are PIREPs (UA), and where are they usually found? (AC 00-45E)

These reports contain information concerning weather as observed by pilots en route. Required elements for all PIREPs are message type, location, time (in UTC), flight level (altitudes are MSL), type of aircraft, and at least one weather element encountered (visibility in SM, distances in NM). A PIREP (abbreviation for "pilot reports") is usually transmitted as an individual report but can be appended to a surface aviation weather report or placed into collectives. Also referred to in coded reported as "UA."

5. What are Radar Weather Reports (SD)? (AC 00-45E)

General areas of precipitation, including rain, snow, and thunderstorms, can be observed by radar. The radar weather report (SD) includes the type, intensity, and location of the echo top of the precipitation. All heights are reported above MSL. Radar stations report each hour at H+35. SDs should be used along with METARs, satellite photos, and forecasts when planning a flight, to help in thunderstorm area avoidance. But once airborne, depend on Flight Watch, which has the capability to display current radar images, airborne radar, or visual sighting to evade individual storms.

D. Aviation Weather Forecasts

1. What are Terminal Aerodrome Forecasts (TAFs)? (AC 00-45E)

An Aviation Terminal Forecast (TAF) is a concise statement of the expected meteorological conditions within a 5-SM radius from the center of an airport's runway complex during a 24-hour time period. The TAFs use the same weather code found in METAR weather reports, in the following format:

a. *Type of reports* — a routine forecast (TAF); and an amended forecast, TAF AMD.

b. *ICAO station identifier* — 4-letter station identifiers.

c. *Date and time of origin* — the date and UTC the forecast is actually prepared; 2-digit date, and 4-digit time, (no space) followed by the letter Z.

Continued

d. *Valid period date and time* — valid forecast period is a 2-digit date followed by the 2-digit beginning and 2-digit ending hours in UTC. Routine TAFs are valid for 24 hours and are issued four times daily at 0000Z, 0600Z, 1200Z, and 1800Z.

e. *Forecasts* — wind, significant weather, sky condition, nonconvective low-level wind shear, change indicators, probability.

2. What is an Aviation Area Forecast (FA)? (AC 00-45E)

A forecast of visual meteorological conditions (VMC), clouds, and general weather conditions over an area the size of several states. To understand the complete weather picture, the FA must be used along with inflight weather advisories to determine forecast enroute weather and to interpolate conditions at airports where no TAFs are issued. FAs are issued 3 times a day by the Aviation Weather Center (AWC) for each of the 6 areas in the contiguous 48 states. The weather forecast office (WFO) in Honolulu issues FAs for Hawaii. The Alaska Aviation Weather Unit (AAWU) in Anchorage, Alaska produces the FA for the entire state of Alaska. There are also two specialized FAs, one for the Gulf of Mexico, and one for international airspace.

3. What information is provided by an Aviation Area Forecast (FA)? (AC 00-45E)

The FA is comprised of four sections:

a. *Communications and product header section* — identifies the office from which the FA is issued, the date and time of issue, the product name, the valid times and the states and/or areas covered by the FA.

b. *Precautionary statement section* — between the communications/products headers and the body of the forecast are three precautionary statements which are in all Area Forecasts:

SEE AIRMET SIERRA FOR IFR CONDITIONS AND MTN OBSC

This alerts user that IFR conditions and/or mountain obscurement may be occurring or may be forecast to occur in a portion of the FA area.

TSTMS IMPLY PSBL SVR OR GTR TURBC SVR ICG
LLWS AND IFR CONDS
> A reminder of the hazards existing in all thunderstorms.

NON MSL HGTS ARE DENOTED BY AGL OR CIG
> This alerts user that heights, for the most part, are heights
> above sea level. All heights are in hundreds of feet. The tops
> of clouds, turbulence, icing and freezing level heights are
> always MSL. Heights above ground level are noted in either
> of the following ways: ceilings by definition are above
> ground; therefore, the contraction "CIG" indicates above
> ground. The contraction "AGL" means above ground level;
> thus, if the contraction "AGL" or "CIG" is not denoted,
> height is automatically above MSL.

c. *Synopsis section*—a brief summary of the location and movements of fronts, pressure systems, and circulation patterns for
an 18-hour period. References to low ceilings and/or visibilities, strong winds, or any other phenomena the forecaster considers useful, may also be included.

d. *VFR Clouds and Weather section*—contains a 12-hour specific
forecast, followed by a six-hour (18-hour in Alaska) categorical
outlook giving a total forecast period of 18 hours (30 hours in
Alaska). The VFR CLDS/WX section is usually several para-
graphs long. The breakdown may be by states or by well-
known geographical areas. The specific forecast section gives a
general description of clouds and weather which cover an area
greater than 3,000 square miles and is significant to VFR flight
operations.

4. What are Inflight Aviation Weather Advisories (WST, WS, WA)? (AC 00-45E)

Inflight aviation weather advisories are forecasts to advise enroute
aircraft of development of potentially hazardous weather, in 3
types: the SIGMET, AIRMET, and Convective SIGMET. All
heights are referenced MSL, except in the case of ceilings CIG,
which indicate AGL.

5. What is a Convective SIGMET? (AC 00-45E)

Convective SIGMETs (WST) implies severe or greater turbulence, severe icing and low-level wind shear. They may be issued for any convective situation which the forecaster feels is hazardous to all categories of aircraft. Convective SIGMET bulletins are issued for the Eastern (E), Central (C) and Western (W) United States (Convective SIGMETs are not issued for Alaska or Hawaii). Bulletins are issued hourly at H+55. Special bulletins are issued at any time as required and updated at H+55. The text of the bulletin consists of either an observation and a forecast, or just a forecast. The forecast is valid for up to 2 hours.

a. Severe thunderstorm due to:
   - Surface winds greater than or equal to 50 knots.
   - Hail at the surface greater than or equal to $\frac{3}{4}$ inches in diameter.
   - Tornadoes

b. Embedded thunderstorms

c. A line of thunderstorms

d. Thunderstorms producing greater than or equal to heavy precipitation that affects 40% or more of an area at least 3,000 square miles.

6. What is a SIGMET (WS)? (AC 00-45E)

A SIGMET (WS) advises of non-convective weather that is potentially hazardous to all aircraft. SIGMETs are issued for the six areas corresponding to the FA areas. The maximum forecast period is four hours. In the conterminous U.S., SIGMETs are issued when the following phenomena occur or are expected to occur:

a. Severe icing not associated with a thunderstorm;

b. Severe or extreme turbulence or clear air turbulence (CAT) not associated with thunderstorms;

c. Duststorms or sandstorms lowering surface or inflight visibilities to below 3 miles;

d. Volcanic ash.

7. What is an AIRMET (WA)? (AC 00-45E)

Advisories of significant weather phenomena that describe conditions at intensities lower than those which require the issuance of SIGMETs, intended for use by all pilots in the preflight and enroute phase of flight to enhance safety. AIRMET Bulletins are issued every 6 hours beginning at 0145 UTC during Central Daylight Time and at 0245 UTC during Central Standard Time. Unscheduled updates and corrections are issued as necessary.

Each AIRMET Bulletin includes an outlook for conditions expected after the AIRMET valid period. AIRMETs contain details about IFR, extensive mountain obscuration, turbulence, strong surface winds, icing, and freezing levels.

8. What is a TWEB? (AC 00-45E)

NWS offices prepare transcribed weather broadcast (TWEB) text products for the contiguous U.S., including synopsis and forecast for more than 200 routes and local vicinities. TWEB products are valid for 12 hours and are issued 4 times a day at 0200Z, 0800Z, 1400Z, and 2000Z in a variety of sources (TIBS, PATWAS, and more).

A TWEB route forecast or vicinity forecast will not be issued if the TAF for that airport has not been issued. A TWEB route forecast is for a 50-NM wide corridor along a line connecting the end points of the route. A TWEB local vicinity forecast covers an area with a radius of 50 NM. These forecasts describe sustained surface winds (25 knots or greater), visibility, weather and obscuration to vision, sky conditions (coverage and ceiling/cloud heights), mountain obscurement, and nonconvective low-level wind shear.

9. What is a Winds and Temperatures Aloft Forecast (FD)? (AC 00-45E)

Winds and temperatures aloft are forecasted for specific locations in the contiguous U.S., and also prepared for a network of locations in Alaska and Hawaii. Forecasts are made twice daily based on the 00Z and 12Z radiosonde data for use during specific time intervals. FDs contain the following characteristics:

a. The valid time period the FD may be used, and a notation "TEMPS NEG ABV 24000." Since temperatures above 24,000 feet are always negative, the minus sign is omitted.

b. "FT" indicates the levels of the wind and temperature data. Through 12,000, feet the levels are true altitude. From 18,000 feet and above, the levels are pressure altitude.

c. A 4-digit group shows wind direction in tens of degrees, and the second 2 digits are the wind speed in knots. A 6-digit group includes forecast temperatures in degrees Celsius.

d. No winds are forecasted within 1,500 feet of station elevation.

e. No temperatures are forecasted for any level within 2,500 feet of station elevation.

f. If a wind direction is coded between 51 and 86, the wind speed is 100 knots or greater. For example, winds forecast for 39,000 feet indicate "731960." To decode, subtract 50 from the wind direction and add 100 knots to the wind speed. Wind direction is from 230 degrees (73–50=23); speed is 119 knots (100+19=119) and temperature is -60°C.

g. If the wind speed is forecasted to be 200 knots or greater, the wind group is coded as 99 knots. For example, "7799" is decoded as 270 degrees at 199 knots or greater.

h. When the forecast speed is less than 5 knots, the coded group is "9900" which means, "Light and Variable."

10. **What valuable information can be determined from Winds and Temperatures Aloft Forecasts (FD)?** (AC 00-45E)

Most favorable altitude—based on winds and direction of flight.

Areas of possible icing—by noting air temperatures of +2°C to -20°C.

Temperature inversions.

Turbulence—by observing abrupt changes in wind direction and speed at different altitudes.

11. **What are Center Weather Advisories (CWA)?** (AC 00-45E)

A Center Weather Advisory (CWA) is an aviation warning for use by aircrews to anticipate and avoid adverse weather conditions in the en route and terminal environments. The CWA is not a flight planning product; instead it reflects current conditions expected at the time of issuance and/or is a short-range forecast for conditions expected to begin within 2 hours of issuance. CWAs are valid for a maximum of 2 hours. If conditions are expected to continue beyond the 2-hour valid period, a statement will be included in the CWA.

12. **What is a Convective Outlook (AC)?** (AC 00-45E)

A national forecast of thunderstorms, in 2 parts: Day 1 Convective Outlook (first 24 hours), and Day 2 Convective Outlook (next 24 hours). Describe areas in which there is a slight, moderate, or high risk of severe thunderstorms, as well as areas of general (non-severe) thunderstorms. The times of issuance for Day 1 are 0600Z, 1300Z, 1630Z, 2000Z, and 0100Z. The initial Day 2 issuance is at 0830Z during standard time and 0730Z during daylight time, updated at 1730Z. The AC is a flight planning tool used to avoid thunderstorms.

E. Aviation Weather Charts

1. Give some examples of current weather charts available at the FSS or NWSO used in flight planning. (AC 00-45E)

a. Surface Analysis Chart

b. Weather Depiction Chart

c. Radar Summary Chart

d. Significant Weather Prognostic Chart

e. Winds and Temperatures Aloft Chart

f. Composite Moisture Stability Chart

g. Convective Outlook Chart

h. Constant Pressure Analysis Chart

i. Volcanic Ash Forecast Transport and Dispersion Chart

2. What is a Surface Analysis Chart? (AC 00-45E)

This is a computer-prepared chart that covers the contiguous 48 states and adjacent areas. The chart is transmitted every three hours. The surface analysis chart provides a ready means of locating pressure systems and fronts. It also gives an overview of winds, temperatures and dew point temperatures at chart time. When using the chart, keep in mind that weather moves and conditions change. Using the surface analysis chart in conjunction with other information gives a more complete weather picture.

3. What information does a Weather Depiction Chart provide? (AC 00-45E)

The weather depiction chart is computer-generated (with a weather observer's analysis of fronts) from METAR reports. This chart gives a broad overview of the observed flying category conditions at the valid time of the chart. The chart begins at 01Z each day, is transmitted at three-hour intervals, and is valid at the time of the plotted data. The plotted data for each station area are: total sky cover, cloud height or ceiling, weather and obstructions to vision and visibilities. The weather depiction chart is an ideal place to begin in preparing for a weather briefing and flight planning. From this chart one can get a "bird's-eye" view of areas of favorable and adverse weather conditions at chart time.

4. Define the terms: IFR, MVFR and VFR. (AC 00-45E)

IFR: Ceilings less than 1,000 and/or visibilities less than 3 miles (Instrument Flight Rules)

MVFR: (Marginal VFR) Ceiling 1,000 to 3,000 feet inclusive and/or visibility 3 to 5 miles inclusive

VFR: No ceiling, or ceiling greater than 3,000 and visibility greater than 5 miles (Visual Flight Rules)

5. What are Radar Summary Charts? (AC 00-45E)

Computer-generated graphical display of a collection of auto-mated radar weather reports (SDs). The chart displays areas of precipitation as well as information about type, intensity, configu-ration, coverage, echo top, and cell movement of precipitation. Severe weather watches are plotted if they are in effect when the chart is valid. The chart is available hourly with a valid time of 35 minutes past each hour.

This chart aids in preflight planning by identifying general areas and movement of precipitation and/or thunderstorms. Dis-plays drops or ice particles of precipitation size only; it does not display clouds and fog. Therefore, since the absence of echoes does not guarantee clear weather, and cloud tops will most likely be higher than the tops of the precipitation echoes detected by radar, the radar summary chart must be used along with other charts, reports, and forecasts for best effectiveness.

6. What are Significant Weather Prognostic Charts? (AC 00-45E)

Called "progs," these charts portray forecasts of selected weather conditions at specified valid times (12, 24, 36, and 48 hour progs). Each valid time is the time at which the forecast conditions are expected to occur, made from a comprehensive set of observed weather conditions. The observed conditions are extended forward in time and become forecasts by considering atmospheric and en-vironmental processes. Forecast information for the surface to 24,000 feet is provided by the low-level significant weather prog chart. Forecast information from above 24,000 to 60,000 feet is provided by the high-level significant weather prog chart.

7. **Describe a U.S. Low-Level Significant Weather Prog Chart.** (AC 00-45E)

It is a "Day One" forecast of significant weather for the contermi-nous U.S., pertaining to the layer from surface to FL240 (400 mb). With two forecast periods, 12 hours and 24 hours, the chart is com-posed of four panels. The two lower panels depict the 12- and 24-hour surface progs, and the two upper panels depict the 12- and 24-hour significant weather progs. Issued four times a day at 00Z, 06Z, 12Z, and 18Z. Covered are forecast positions and characteris-tics of pressure systems, fronts, and precipitation. Much insight can be gained by evaluating the individual fields of pressure patterns, fronts, precipitation, weather flying categories, freezing levels, and turbulence displayed on the chart.

8. **What is a Forecast Winds and Temperatures Aloft Chart (FD)?** (AC 00-45E)

This chart is a computer-generated chart depicting both observed and forecast winds and temperatures aloft. Forecast winds and tem-peratures aloft are prepared for eight levels on eight separate pan-els. The levels are 6,000, 9,000, 12,000, 18,000, 24,000, 30,000, 34,000 and 39,000 feet MSL. They are available daily as 12-hour progs valid at 1200Z and 0000Z. These charts are typically used to determine winds at a proposed altitude or to select the best altitude for a proposed flight. Temperatures also can be determined from the forecast charts. Interpolation must be used to determine winds and temperatures at a level between charts and data when the time period is other than the valid time of the chart.

9. **What is a Composite Moisture Stability Chart?** (AC 00-45E)

This is an analysis chart using observed upper air data. The chart is composed of four panels including stability, freezing level, pre-cipitable water and, average relative humidity. This computer-generated chart is available twice daily with valid times of 12Z and 00Z. It is used to determine the characteristics of a particular weather system in terms of stability, moisture, and possible avia-tion hazards. Generally, these characteristics tend to move with the associated weather systems, such as lows, highs, and fronts. Exer-cise caution, as modification of these characteristics could occur through development, dissipation, or the movement of the system.

10. What is a Convective Outlook Chart? (AC 00-45E)

This chart depicts areas forecast to have thunderstorms, and is presented in two panels. The left-hand panel is the Day 1 Convective Outlook, and the right-hand panel is the Day 2 Convective Outlook. "Day 1" outlines areas in the continental U.S. where thunderstorms are forecasted during that period. It is issued five times daily (0600Z, 1300Z, 1630Z, 2000Z, and 0100Z) and all issuances are valid until 12Z the following day. The outlook issued qualifies the level of risk (i.e., SLGT, MDT, HIGH) as well as the areas of general thunderstorms.

The Day 2 Convective Outlook contains the same information as the Day 1 chart, and is issued twice a day (0830Z and 1730Z) in a period from 12Z the following day to 12Z the next day.

11. What are Constant Pressure Analysis Charts?
(AC 00-45E)

Any surface of equal pressure in the atmosphere is a constant pressure surface. A constant pressure analysis chart is an upper air weather map where all information depicted is at the specified pressure of the chart. From these charts, a pilot can approximate the observed air temperature, wind, and temperature-dewpoint spread along a proposed route. They also depict highs, lows, troughs, and ridges aloft by the height contour patterns resembling isobars on a surface map. Twice daily, six computer-prepared constant pressure charts are transmitted by facsimile for six pressure levels:

850 mb .... 5,000 ft
700 mb .... 10,000 ft
500 mb .... 18,000 ft
300 mb .... 30,000 ft
250 mb .... 34,000 ft
200 mb .... 39,000 ft

12. Describe a Volcanic Ash Forecast Transport and Dispersion Chart. (AC 00-45E)

This VAFTAD chart presents the relative concentrations of ash following a volcanic eruption for three layers of the atmosphere in addition to a composite of ash concentration through the atmosphere. The chart focuses on hazards to aircraft flight operations caused by volcanic eruption with an emphasis on the ash cloud location in time and space. It uses National Centers for Environmental Prediction forecast data to determine the location of ash concentrations over 6-hour and 12-hour time intervals. The chart is strictly for advanced flight planning purposes. It is not intended to take the place of SIGMETs regarding volcanic eruptions and ash.

Additional Study Questions

1. **How can a pilot receive updated weather information inflight?** (AIM 7-1-5)

2. **Decode the following pilot weather report (PIREP):** (AIM 7-1-21)

   KCMH UA/OV KAPE 230010/TM 1516/FL085/TP BE20/SK BKN 065/WX FV03SM HZ FU/TA 20/TB LGT

3. **Decode the following Terminal Aerodrome Forecast (TAF):** (AIM 7-1-30)

   TAF KPIT 091730Z 091818 15005KT 5SM HZ FEW020 WS010/31022KT

   FM1930 30015G25KT 3SM SHRA OVC015 TEMPO 2022 1/2SM +TSRA OVC008CB

   FM0100 27008KT 5SM SHRA BKN020 OVC040 PROB40 0407 1SM -RA BR

   FM1015 18005KT 6SM -SHRA OVC020 BECMG 1315 P6SM NSW SKC

4. What symbols are used to depict the following frontal systems on surface analysis charts? Cold, Warm, Stationary, Occluded. (AC 00-6A)

5. What is a microburst? When and where are they most likely to occur? (AIM 7-1-26)

6. What is a sea breeze, and why does it occur? (AC 00-6A)

7. What is a mountain wave? (AC 00-6A)

8. Define the term "ceiling." (AC 00-6A)

9. Give some examples of charts and reports useful in determining the potential for and location of thunderstorms along your route. (AC 00-45E)

10. If your destination has no Terminal Forecast, which primary source of information should be referenced for forecasted weather at the estimated time of arrival? (AC 00-45E)

Determining Performance and Limitations

3

A. Aerodynamics

1. What are the four dynamic forces that act on an airplane during all maneuvers? (FAA-H-8083-25)

Lift—the upward acting force

Gravity—or weight, the downward acting force

Thrust—the forward acting force

Drag—the backward acting force

2. What flight condition will result in the sum of the opposing forces being equal? (FAA-H-8083-25)

In steady-state, straight-and-level, unaccelerated flight, the sum of the opposing forces is equal to zero. There can be no unbalanced forces in steady, straight flight (Newton's Third Law). This is true whether flying level or when climbing or descending. This simply means that the opposing forces are equal to, and thereby cancel the effects of, each other.

3. What is an airfoil? State some examples. (FAA-H-8083-25)

An airfoil is a device which gets a useful reaction from air moving over its surface, namely LIFT. Wings, horizontal tail surfaces, vertical tail surfaces, and propellers are examples of airfoils.

4. What is the "angle of incidence"? (FAA-H-8083-25)

The angle of incidence is the angle formed by the longitudinal axis of the airplane and the chord of the wing. It is measured by the angle at which the wing is attached to the fuselage. The angle of incidence is fixed and cannot be changed by the pilot.

5. What is a "relative wind"? (FAA-H-8083-25)

The relative wind is the direction of the airflow with respect to the wing. When a wing is moving forward and downward the relative wind moves backward and upward. The flight path and relative wind are always parallel but travel in opposite directions.

6. What is the "angle of attack"? (FAA-H-8083-25)

The angle of attack is the angle between the wing chord line and the direction of the relative wind; it can be changed by the pilot.

7. What is "Bernoulli's Principle"? (FAA-H-8083-25)

Bernoulli's Principle—The pressure of a fluid (liquid or gas) decreases at points where the speed of the fluid increases. In the case of airflow, high speed flow is associated with low pressure and low speed flow with high pressure. The airfoil of an aircraft is designed to increase the velocity of the airflow above its surface, thereby decreasing pressure above the airfoil. Simultaneously, the impact of the air on the lower surface of the airfoil increases the pressure below. This combination of pressure decrease above and increase below produces lift.

8. What are several factors which will affect both lift and drag?

Wing area—Lift and drag acting on a wing are roughly proportional to the wing area. A pilot can change wing area by using certain types of flaps (i.e., Fowler flaps).

Shape of the airfoil—As the upper curvature of an airfoil is increased (up to a certain point) the lift produced increases. Lowering an aileron or flap device can accomplish this. Also, ice or frost on a wing can disturb normal airflow, changing its camber, and disrupting its lifting capability.

Angle of attack—As angle of attack is increased, both lift and drag are increased, up to a certain point.

Velocity of the air—An increase in velocity of air passing over the wing increases lift and drag.

Air density—Lift and drag vary directly with the density of the air. As air density increases, lift and drag increase. As air density decreases, lift and drag decrease. Air density is affected by these factors: pressure, temperature, and humidity.

9. What is "torque effect"? (FAA-H-8083-25)

Torque effect involves Newton's Third Law of Physics—for every action, there is an equal and opposite reaction. Applied to the airplane, this means that as the internal engine parts and the propeller are revolving in one direction, an equal force is trying to rotate the airplane in the opposite direction. It is greatest when at low airspeeds with high power settings and a high angle of attack.

10. What effect does torque reaction have on an airplane on the ground and in flight? (FAA-H-8083-25)

In flight—torque reaction is acting around the longitudinal axis, tending to make the airplane roll. To compensate, some of the older airplanes are rigged in a manner to create more lift on the wing that is being forced downward. The more modern airplanes are designed with the engine offset to counteract this effect of torque.

On the ground—during the takeoff roll, an additional turning moment around the vertical axis is induced by torque reaction. As the left side of the airplane is being forced down by torque reaction, more weight is being placed on the left main landing gear. This results in more ground friction, or drag, on the left tire than on the right, causing a further turning moment to the left.

11. What are the four factors that contribute to torque effect? (FAA-H-8083-25)

Torque reaction of the engine and propeller. For every action there is an equal and opposite reaction. The rotation of the propeller (from the cockpit) to the right, tends to roll or bank the airplane to the left.

Gyroscopic effect of the propeller. Gyroscopic precession applies here: the resultant action or deflection of a spinning object when a force is applied to the outer rim of its rotational mass. If the axis of a propeller is tilted, the resulting force will be exerted 90° ahead in the direction of rotation and in the same direction as the applied force. It is most noticeable on takeoffs in taildraggers when the tail is raised.

Continued

Corkscrewing effect of the propeller slipstream. High-speed rotation of an airplane propeller results in a corkscrewing rotation to the slipstream as it moves rearward. At high propeller speeds and low forward speeds (as in a takeoff), the slipstream strikes the vertical tail surface on the left side pushing the tail to the right and yawing the airplane to the left.

Asymmetrical loading of the propeller (P-Factor). When an airplane is flying with a high angle of attack, the bite of the downward moving propeller blade is greater than the bite of the upward moving blade. This is due to the downward moving blade meeting the oncoming relative wind at a greater angle of attack than the upward moving blade. Consequently there is greater thrust on the downward moving blade on the right side, and this forces the airplane to yaw to the left.

12. What is "centrifugal force"? (FAA-H-8083-25)

Centrifugal force is the "equal and opposite reaction" of the airplane to the change in direction, and it acts "equal and opposite" to the horizontal component of lift.

13. What is "load factor"? (FAA-H-8083-25)

Load factor is the ratio of the total load supported by the airplane's wing to the actual weight of the airplane and its contents. In other words, it is the actual load supported by the wings divided by the total weight of the airplane. It can also be expressed as the ratio of a given load to the pull of gravity; i.e., to refer to a load factor of three as "3 Gs." In this case the weight of the airplane is equal to 1 G, and if a load of three times the actual weight of the airplane were imposed upon the wing due to curved flight, the load factor would be equal to 3 Gs.

14. For what two reasons is load factor important to pilots? (FAA-H-8083-25)

a. Because of the obviously dangerous overload that it is possible for a pilot to impose on the aircraft structure.

b. Because an increased load factor increases the stalling speed and makes stalls possible at seemingly safe flight speeds.

15. What situations may result in load factors reaching the maximum or being exceeded? (FAA-H-8083-25)

Level Turns — The load factor increases at a terrific rate after a bank has reached 45° or 50°. The load factor in a 60°-bank turn is 2 Gs. The load factor in a 80°-bank turn is 5.76 Gs. The wing must produce lift equal to these load factors if altitude is to be maintained.

Turbulence — Severe vertical gusts cause a sudden increase in angle of attack, resulting in large loads which are resisted by the inertia of the airplane.

Speed — The amount of excess load that can be imposed upon the wing depends on how fast the airplane is flying. At speeds below maneuvering speed, the airplane will stall before the load factor can become excessive. At speeds above maneuvering speed, the limit load factor for which an airplane is stressed can be exceeded by abrupt or excessive application of the controls or by strong turbulence.

16. What are the different operational categories for aircraft and within which category does your aircraft fall? (FAA-H-8083-25)

The maximum safe load factors (limit load factors) specified for airplanes in the various categories are as follows:

a. Normal .... +3.8 to -1.52
b. Utility (mild aerobatics including spins) .... +4.4 to -1.76
c. Aerobatic .... +6.0 to -3.00

17. What effect does an increase in load factor have on stalling speed? (FAA-H-8083-25)

As load factor increases, stalling speed increases. Any airplane can be stalled at any airspeed within the limits of its structure and the strength of the pilot. At a given airspeed the load factor increases as angle of attack increases, and the wing stalls because the angle of attack has been increased to a certain angle. Therefore, there is a direct relationship between the load factor imposed upon the wing and its stalling characteristics. A rule for determining the speed at which a wing will stall is that the stalling speed increases in proportion to the square root of the load factor.

18. Define the term "maneuvering speed." (FAA-H-8083-3)

Maneuvering speed is the maximum speed at which abrupt control movement can be applied or at which the airplane could be flown in turbulence without exceeding design load factor limits. When operating below this speed, a damaging positive flight load should not be produced because the airplane should stall before the load becomes excessive.

19. Discuss the effect on maneuvering speed of an increase or decrease in weight. (FAA-H-8083-25)

Maneuvering speed increases with an increase in weight and decreases with a decrease in weight. An aircraft operating at a reduced weight is more vulnerable to rapid accelerations encountered during flight through turbulence or gusts. Design limit load factors could be exceeded if a reduction in maneuvering speed is not accomplished. An aircraft operating at or near gross weight in turbulent air is much less likely to exceed design limit load factors and may be operated at the published maneuvering speed for gross weight if necessary.

20. What causes an airplane to stall? (FAA-H-8083-25)

An airplane stalls when the critical angle of attack has been exceeded. When the angle of attack increases to approximately 18° to 20°, the air can no longer flow smoothly over the top wing surface. Because the airflow cannot make such a great change in direction so quickly, it becomes impossible for the air to follow the contour of the wing. This is the stalling or critical angle of attack. This can occur at any airspeed, in any attitude, with any power setting.

21. What is a "spin"? (AC 61-67C)

A spin in a small airplane or glider is a controlled (recoverable) or uncontrolled (possibly unrecoverable) maneuver in which the airplane or glider descends in a helical path while flying at an angle of attack greater than the critical angle of attack. Spins result from aggravated stalls in either a slip or a skid. If a stall does not occur, a spin cannot occur.

22. What causes a spin? (AC 61-67C)

The primary cause of an inadvertent spin is exceeding the critical angle of attack while applying excessive or insufficient rudder, and to a lesser extent, aileron.

23. When are spins most likely to occur? (AC 61-67C)

A stall/spin situation can occur in any phase of flight but is most likely to occur in the following situations:

a. *Engine failure on takeoff during climbout*—pilot tries to stretch glide to landing area by increasing back pressure or makes an uncoordinated turn back to departure runway at a relatively low airspeed.

b. *Crossed-control turn from base to final (slipping or skidding turn)*—pilot overshoots final (possibly due to a crosswind) and makes uncoordinated turn at a low airspeed.

c. *Engine failure on approach to landing*—pilot tries to stretch glide to runway by increasing back pressure.

d. *Go-around with full nose-up trim*—pilot applies power with full flaps and nose-up trim combined with uncoordinated use of rudder.

e. *Go-around with improper flap retraction*—pilot applies power and retracts flaps rapidly resulting in a rapid sink rate followed by an instinctive increase in back pressure.

24. What procedure should be used to recover from an inadvertent spin? (AC 61-67C)

a. Close the throttle (if not already accomplished).

b. Neutralize the ailerons.

c. Apply full opposite rudder.

d. Briskly move the elevator control forward to approximately the neutral position. (Some aircraft require merely a relaxation of back pressure; others require full forward elevator pressure).

e. Once the stall is broken the spinning will stop. Neutralize the rudder when the spinning stops.

f. When the rudder is neutralized, gradually apply enough aft elevator pressure to return to level flight.

25. What causes "adverse yaw"? (FAA-H-8083-25)

When turning an airplane to the left for example, the downward deflected aileron on the right produces more lift on the right wing. Since the downward deflected right aileron produces more lift, it also produces more drag, while the opposite left aileron has less lift and less drag. This added drag attempts to pull or veer the airplane's nose in the direction of the raised wing (right); that is, it tries to turn the airplane in the direction opposite to that desired. This undesired veering is referred to as adverse yaw.

26. What is "ground effect"? (FAA-H-8083-3)

Ground effect is a condition of improved performance the airplane experiences when it is operating near the ground. A change occurs in the three-dimensional flow pattern around the airplane because the airflow around the wing is restricted by the ground surface. This reduces the wing's upwash, downwash, and wingtip vortices. In order for ground effect to be of a significant magnitude, the wing must be quite close to the ground.

27. What major problems can be caused by ground effect? (FAA-H-8083-3)

During landing, at a height of approximately one-tenth of a wing span above the surface, drag may be 40 percent less than when the airplane is operating out of ground effect. Therefore, any excess speed during the landing phase may result in a significant float distance. In such cases, if care is not exercised by the pilot, he/she may run out of runway and options at the same time.

During takeoff, due to the reduced drag in ground effect, the aircraft may seem capable of takeoff well below the recommended speed. However, as the airplane rises out of ground effect with a deficiency of speed, the greater induced drag may result in very marginal climb performance, or the inability of the airplane to fly at all. In extreme conditions, such as high temperature, high gross weight, and high-density altitude, the airplane may become airborne initially with a deficiency of speed and then settle back to the runway.

B. Weight and Balance

1. Define the following: (FAA-H-8083-25)

Empty weight—The airframe, engines, and all items of operating equipment that have fixed locations and are permanently installed in the aircraft. Includes hydraulic fluid, unusable fuel, and undrainable oil.

Gross weight—The maximum allowable weight of both the airplane and its contents.

Useful load—The weight of the pilot, copilot, passengers, baggage, usable fuel and drainable oil.

Arm—The horizontal distance in inches from the reference datum line to the center of gravity of the item.

Moment—The product of the weight of an item multiplied by its arm. Moments are expressed in pound-inches.

Center of gravity—The point about which an aircraft would balance if it were possible to suspend it at that point. Expressed in inches from datum.

Datum—An imaginary vertical plane or line from which all measurements of arm are taken. Established by the manufacturer.

2. What basic equation is used in all weight and balance problems to find the center of gravity location of an airplane and/or its components? (FAA-H-8083-25)

Weight x Arm = Moment

By rearrangement of this equation to the forms:

Weight = Moment ÷ Arm

$$\text{Arm (CG)} = \frac{\text{(Total) Moment}}{\text{(Total) Weight}}$$

With any two known values, the third value can be found.

Remember: W A M
(Weight x Arm = Moment)

3. **What performance characteristics will be adversely affected when an aircraft has been overloaded?** (FAA-H-8083-1)

   a. Higher takeoff speed

   b. Longer takeoff run

   c. Reduced rate and angle of climb

   d. Lower maximum altitude

   e. Shorter range

   f. Reduced cruising speed

   g. Reduced maneuverability

   h. Higher stalling speed

   i. Higher landing speed

   j. Longer landing roll

   k. Excessive weight on the nosewheel

4. **What effect does a forward center of gravity have on an aircraft's flight characteristics?** (FAA-H-8083-1)

   Higher stall speed—stalling angle of attack is reached at a higher speed due to increased wing loading.

   Slower cruise speed—increased drag; greater angle of attack is required to maintain altitude.

   More stable—the center of gravity is farther forward from the center of pressure which increases longitudinal stability.

   Greater back elevator pressure required—longer takeoff roll; higher approach speeds and problems with landing flare.

5. **What effect does a rearward center of gravity have on an aircraft's flight characteristics?** (FAA-H-8083-1)

   Lower stall speed—less wing loading.

   Higher cruise speed—reduced drag; smaller angle of attack is required to maintain altitude.

   Less stable—stall and spin recovery more difficult; the center of gravity is closer to the center of pressure, causing longitudinal instability.

6. What are the standard weights assumed for the following when calculating weight and balance problems? (FAA-H-8083-25)

Crew and passengers .... 170 lbs each

Gasoline .... 6 lbs/U.S. gal

Oil .... 7.5 lbs/U.S. gal

Water .... 8.35 lbs/U.S. gal

C. Aircraft Performance

1. What are some of the main elements of aircraft performance? (FAA-H-8083-25)

   a. Takeoff and landing distance

   b. Rate of climb

   c. Ceiling

   d. Payload

   e. Range

   f. Speed

   g. Fuel economy

2. What factors affect the performance of an aircraft during takeoffs and landings? (FAA-H-8083-25)

   a. Air density (density altitude)

   b. Surface wind

   c. Runway surface

   d. Upslope or downslope of runway

   e. Weight

3. What effect does wind have on aircraft performance? (FAA-H-8083-25)

Takeoff—a headwind will increase the airplane performance by shortening the takeoff distance and increasing the angle of climb. However, a tailwind will decrease performance by increasing the takeoff distance and reducing the angle of climb. The decrease in airplane performance must be carefully considered by the pilot before a downwind takeoff is attempted.

Landing—a headwind will increase airplane performance by steepening the approach angle and reducing the landing distance. A tailwind will decrease performance by decreasing the approach angle and increasing the landing distance. Again, the pilot must take the wind into consideration prior to landing.

Cruise flight—winds aloft have somewhat an opposite effect on airplane performance. A headwind will decrease performance by reducing ground speed, which in turn increases the fuel requirement for the flight. A tailwind will increase performance by increasing the ground speed, which in turn reduces the fuel requirement for the flight.

4. How does weight affect takeoff and landing performance? (FAA-H-8083-25)

Increased gross weight can have a significant effect on takeoff performance:

a. Higher liftoff speed;

b. Greater mass to accelerate (slow acceleration);

c. Increased retarding force (drag and ground friction); and

d. Longer takeoff distance.

The effect of gross weight on landing distance is that the airplane will require a greater speed to support the airplane at the landing angle of attack and lift coefficient resulting in an increased landing distance.

5. **What effect does an increase in density altitude have on takeoff and landing performance?** (FAA-P-8740-2)

An increase in density altitude results in:

a. Increased takeoff distance (greater takeoff TAS required).

b. Reduced rate of climb (decreased thrust and reduced acceleration)

c. Increased true airspeed on approach and landing (same IAS).

d. Increased landing roll distance.

6. **Define the term "density altitude."** (FAA-H-8083-25)

Density altitude is pressure altitude corrected for nonstandard temperature. Under standard atmospheric condition, air at each level in the atmosphere has a specific density, and under standard conditions, pressure altitude and density altitude identify the same level. Therefore, density altitude is the vertical distance above sea level in the standard atmosphere at which a given density is found.

7. **How does air density affect aircraft performance?** (FAA-H-8083-25)

The density of the air has a direct effect on:

a. Lift produced by the wings;

b. Power output of the engine;

c. Propeller efficiency; and

d. Drag forces

8. **What factors affect air density?** (FAA-P-8740-2)

Altitude — the higher the altitude, the less dense the air.

Temperature — the warmer the air, the less dense it is.

Humidity — more humid air is less dense.

9. How does temperature, altitude, and humidity affect density altitude? (FAA-P-8740-2)

a. Density altitude will increase (low air density) when one or more of the following occurs:
- High air temperature
- High altitude
- High humidity

b. Density altitude will decrease (high air density) when one or more of the following occurs:
- Low air temperature
- Low altitude
- Low humidity

10. Know the following speeds for your airplane!

V_{SO}—Stall speed in landing configuration; the calibrated power-off stalling speed or the minimum steady flight speed at which the airplane is controllable in the landing configuration.

V_S—Stall speed clean or in specified configuration; the calibrated power-off stalling speed or the minimum steady flight speed at which the airplane is controllable in a specified configuration.

V_Y—Best rate-of-climb speed; the calibrated airspeed at which the airplane will obtain the maximum increase in altitude per unit of time. This best rate-of-climb speed normally decreases slightly with altitude.

V_X—Best angle-of-climb speed; the calibrated airspeed at which the airplane will obtain the highest altitude in a given horizontal distance. This best angle-of-climb speed normally increases with altitude.

V_{LE}—Maximum landing gear extension speed; the maximum calibrated airspeed at which the airplane can be safely flown with the landing gear extended. This is a problem involving stability and controllability.

V_{LO}—Maximum landing gear operating speed; the maximum calibrated airspeed at which the landing gear can be safely extended or retracted. This is a problem involving the airloads imposed on the operating mechanism during extension or retraction of the gear.

V_{FE}—Maximum flap extension speed; the highest calibrated airspeed permissible with the wing flaps in a prescribed extended position. This is a problem involving the airloads imposed on the structure of the flaps.

V_A—Maneuvering speed; the calibrated design maneuvering airspeed. This is the maximum speed at which the limit load can be imposed (either by gusts or full deflection of the control surfaces) without causing structural damage.

V_{NO}—Normal operating speed; the maximum calibrated airspeed for normal operation or the maximum structural cruise speed. This is the speed above which exceeding the limit load factor may cause permanent deformation of the airplane structure.

V_{NE} — Never exceed speed; the calibrated airspeed which should *never* be exceeded. If flight is attempted above this speed, structural damage or structural failure may result.

11. What information can you obtain from the following charts? (FAA-H-8083-25)

Takeoff Performance Charts

a. Normal takeoff ground run in feet
b. Obstacle clearance ground run in feet (50 feet)

Climb Performance Charts

a. Rate of climb under various conditions
b. Best climb airspeed under various conditions

Cruise Performance Charts

At various altitudes the following:
a. Recommended power settings
b. Percent brake horsepower
c. Rate of fuel consumption (gal/hr)
d. True airspeed
e. Hours of endurance with full tanks
f. Range in miles

Stall Speed Charts

Stall speeds with different flap settings and bank angles.

Landing Performance Charts

a. Normal landing distance
b. Landing distance to clear a 50-foot obstacle

12. Define the term "pressure altitude," and state why it is important. (FAA-H-8083-25)

Pressure Altitude—the altitude indicated when the altimeter setting window (barometric scale) is adjusted to 29.92. This is the altitude above the standard datum plane, a theoretical plane where air pressure (corrected to 15°C) equals 29.92 in. Hg. Pressure altitude is used to compute density altitude, true altitude, true airspeed, and other performance data.

13. The following questions are designed to provide pilots with a general review of the basic information they should know about their specific airplane before taking a flight check or review.

What is the normal climb-out speed? _____

What is the best rate-of-climb speed? _____

What is the best angle-of-climb speed? _____

What is the maximum flap extension speed? _____

What is the maximum gear extension speed? _____

What is the stall speed in the normal landing configuration?

_____

What is the stall speed in the clean configuration? _____

What is the normal approach-to-land speed? _____

What is maneuvering speed? _____

What is red-line speed? _____

What engine-out glide speed will give you maximum range?

_____

What is the make and horsepower of the engine?

_____ _____

How many usable gallons of fuel can you carry? _____

Where are the fuel tanks located, and what are their capacities?

_____ _____

Where are the fuel vents for your aircraft?

_____

What is the octane rating of the fuel used by your aircraft?

_____

Where are the fuel sumps located on your aircraft? When should you drain them?

_____

What are the minimum and maximum oil capacities?

_____   _____

What weight of oil is being used? _____

What is the maximum oil temperature and pressure?

_____   _____

Is the landing gear fixed, manual, hydraulic or electric? If retractable, what is the backup system for lowering the gear?

_____   _____

What are the nosewheel turning limitations for your aircraft?

_____

What is the maximum allowable/demonstrated crosswind component for the aircraft? _____

How many people will this aircraft carry safely with a full fuel load? _____

What is the maximum allowable weight the aircraft can carry with baggage in the baggage compartment? _____

What takeoff distance is required if a takeoff were made from a sea-level pressure altitude? _____

What is your maximum allowable useful load? _____

Solve a weight and balance problem for the flight you plan to make with one passenger at 170 pounds.

a. Does your load fall within the weight and balance envelope?

_____

b. What is the final gross weight? _____

c. How much fuel can be carried? _____

d. How much baggage can be carried with full fuel? _____

e. Know the function of the various types of antennae on your aircraft. _____

Additional Study Questions

1. Where is the weight and balance data located for your airplane and how can you tell if it is correct? (FAA-H-8083-1)

2. Why are some aircraft not allowed to perform forward slips with flaps extended? (AFM)

3. While enroute, will the CG change as your aircraft uses fuel? (FAA-H-8083-25)

4. What causes an airplane (except a T-tail) to pitch nosedown when power is reduced and controls are not adjusted? (FAA-H-8083-25)

5. Will the indicated airspeed at which an aircraft stalls change as altitude is increased? (FAA-H-8083-25)

6. What is a rule of thumb that may be used to determine TAS? (FAA-H-8083-25)

7. What force causes an airplane to turn? (FAA-H-8083-25)

8. The amount of excess load that can be imposed on the structure of an airplane is dependent on what factor? (FAA-H-8083-25)

9. Define the terms "service ceiling" and "absolute ceiling." What are their values for your aircraft? (FAA-H-8083-25)

10. What are several factors which will affect aircraft performance that are not included on the aircraft performance charts? (FAA-H-8083-25)

Airplane
Systems

The following questions reference the Cessna 152 systems. Be sure to review your aircraft's AFM or POH.

A. Aircraft and Engine Operations

1. What are the four main control surfaces and what are their functions? (FAA-H-8083-25)

Elevators—The elevators control the movement of the airplane about its lateral axis. This motion is called pitch.

Ailerons—The ailerons control the airplane's movement about its longitudinal axis. This motion is called roll.

Rudder—The rudder controls movement of the airplane about its vertical axis. This motion is called yaw.

Trim Tabs—Trim tabs are small, adjustable hinged-surfaces on the aileron, rudder, or elevator control surfaces. They are labor-saving devices that enable the pilot to release manual pressure on the primary control.

2. How are the various flight controls operated? (AFM)

The flight control surfaces are manually actuated through use of either a rod or cable system. A control wheel actuates the ailerons and elevator, and rudder/brake pedals actuate the rudder.

3. What are flaps and what is their function? (FAA-H-8083-25)

The wing flaps are movable panels on the inboard trailing edges of the wings. They are hinged so that they may be extended downward into the flow of air beneath the wings to increase both lift and drag. Their purpose is to permit a slower airspeed and a steeper angle of descent during a landing approach. In some cases, they may also be used to shorten the takeoff distance.

4. Describe the landing gear system on this airplane. (AFM)

The landing gear consists of a tricycle-type system utilizing two main wheels and a steerable nosewheel. Tubular spring steel main gear struts provide main gear shock absorption, while nose gear shock absorption is provided by a combination air/oil shock strut.

5. Describe the braking system on this aircraft. (AFM)

Hydraulically actuated disc-type brakes are utilized on each main gear wheel. A hydraulic line connects each brake to a master cylinder located on each pilot's rudder pedals. By applying pressure to the top of either the pilot's or copilot's set of rudder pedals, the brakes may be applied.

6. How is steering accomplished on the ground? (AFM)

Light airplanes are generally provided with nosewheel steering capabilities through a simple system of mechanical linkage connected to the rudder pedals. When a rudder pedal is depressed, a spring-loaded bungee (push-pull rod) connected to the pivotal portion of a nosewheel strut will turn the nosewheel.

7. What type of engine does your aircraft have? (AFM)

A horizontally opposed four-cylinder, overhead-valve, air-cooled, carbureted engine. The engine is manufactured by Lycoming and rated at 110 HP.

8. What four strokes must occur in each cylinder of a typical four stroke engine in order for it to produce full power? (FAA-H-8083-25)

The four strokes are:

Intake—fuel mixture is drawn into cylinder by downward stroke

Compression—mixture is compressed by upward stroke

Power—spark ignites mixture forcing piston downward and producing power

Exhaust—burned gases pushed out of cylinder by upward stroke

9. What does the carburetor do? (FAA-H-8083-25)

Carburetion may be defined as the process of mixing fuel and air in the correct proportions so as to form a combustible mixture. The carburetor vaporizes liquid fuel into small particles and then mixes it with air. It measures the airflow and meters fuel accordingly.

10. How does the carburetor heat system work? (AFM)

A carburetor heat valve, controlled by the pilot, allows unfiltered, heated air from a shroud located around an exhaust riser or muffler to be directed to the induction air manifold prior to the carburetor. Carburetor heat should be used anytime suspected or known carburetor icing conditions exist.

11. What change occurs to the fuel/air mixture when applying carburetor heat? (FAA-H-8083-25)

Normally, the introduction of heated air into the carburetor will result in a richer mixture. Warm air is less dense, resulting in less air for the same amount of fuel.

12. What does the throttle do? (FAA-H-8083-25)

The throttle allows the pilot to manually control the amount of fuel/air charge entering the cylinders. This in turn regulates the engine speed and power.

13. What does the mixture control do? (FAA-H-8083-25)

It regulates the fuel-to-air ratio. All airplane engines incorporate a device called a mixture control, by which the fuel/air ratio can be controlled by the pilot during flight. The purpose of a mixture control is to prevent the mixture from becoming too rich at high altitudes, due to decreasing air density. It is also used to lean the mixture during cross-country flights to conserve fuel and provide optimum power.

14. What type of ignition system does your airplane have? (AFM)

Engine ignition is provided by two engine-driven magnetos, and two spark plugs per cylinder. The ignition system is completely independent of the aircraft electrical system. The magnetos are engine-driven self-contained units supplying electrical current without using an external source of current. However, before they can produce current, the magnetos must be actuated, as the engine crankshaft is rotated by some other means. To accomplish this, the aircraft battery furnishes electrical power to operate a starter which, through a series of gears, rotates the engine crankshaft. This

Continued

in turn actuates the armature of the magneto to produce the sparks for ignition of the fuel in each cylinder. After the engine starts, the starter system is disengaged, and the battery no longer contributes to the actual operation of the engine.

15. What are the two main advantages of a dual ignition system? (FAA-H-8083-25)

a. Increased safety: in case one system fails the engine may be operated on the other until a landing is safely made.

b. More complete and even combustion of the mixture, and consequently, improved engine performance; i.e., the fuel/air mixture will be ignited on each side of the combustion chamber and burn toward the center.

16. What type of fuel system does your aircraft have? (AFM)

The fuel system is a "gravity feed" system. Using gravity, the fuel flows from two wing fuel tanks to a fuel shutoff valve which, in the "on" position, allows fuel to flow through a strainer and then to the carburetor. From there, the fuel is mixed with air and then flows into the cylinders through the intake manifold tubes.

17. What purpose do fuel tank vents have? (AFM)

As the fuel level in an aircraft fuel tank decreases, a vacuum would be created within the tank which would eventually result in a decreasing fuel flow and finally engine stoppage. Fuel system venting provides a way of replacing fuel with outside air, preventing formation of a vacuum.

18. Does your aircraft use a fuel pump? (AFM)

No, the fuel is transferred from the wing tanks to the carburetor by the "gravity feed" system. The gravity system does not require a fuel pump because the fuel is always under positive pressure to the carburetor. For some aircraft where for some reason it is not possible to place the wings above the carburetor, or for which a greater pressure is required than what gravity feed can supply, it is necessary to utilize engine-driven fuel pumps and auxiliary fuel pumps as backups.

19. What type fuel does your aircraft require (minimum octane rating and color)? (AFM)

The approved fuel grade used is 100LL and the color is blue.

20. Can other types of fuel be used if the specified grade is not available? (FAA-H-8083-25)

Airplane engines are designed to operate using a specific grade of fuel as recommended by the manufacturer. If the proper grade of fuel is not available, it is possible, but not desirable, to use the next higher grade as a substitute. Always reference the aircraft's AFM or POH.

21. What color of dye is added to the following fuel grades: 80, 100, 100LL, Turbine? (FAA-H-8083-25)

Grade	Color
80	Red
100	Green
100LL	Blue
Turbine	Colorless

22. What is the function of the manual primer, and how does it operate? (AFM)

The manual primer's main function is to provide assistance in starting the engine. The primer draws fuel from the fuel strainer and injects it directly into the cylinder intake ports. This usually results in a quicker, more efficient engine start.

23. Describe the electrical system on your aircraft. (AFM)

Electrical energy is provided by a 28-volt, direct-current system powered by an engine-driven 60-amp alternator and a 24-volt battery.

24. How are the circuits for the various electrical accessories within the aircraft protected? (AFM)

Most of the electrical circuits in an airplane are protected from an overload condition by either circuit breakers or fuses or both. Circuit breakers perform the same function as fuses except that when an overload occurs, a circuit breaker can be reset.

25. The electrical system provides power for what equipment in an airplane? (AFM)

Normally, the following:

a. Radio equipment
b. Turn coordinator
c. Fuel gauges
d. Pitot heat
e. Landing light
f. Taxi light
g. Strobe lights
h. Interior lights
i. Instrument lights
j. Position lights
k. Flaps (maybe)
l. Stall warning system (maybe)
m. Oil temperature gauge
n. Electric fuel pump (maybe)

26. What does the ammeter indicate? (AFM)

The ammeter indicates the flow of current, in amperes, from the alternator to the battery or from the battery to the electrical system. With the engine running and master switch on, the ammeter will indicate the charging rate to the battery. If the alternator has gone off-line and is no longer functioning, or the electrical load exceeds the output of the alternator, the ammeter indicates the discharge rate of the battery.

27. What function does the voltage regulator have?

The voltage regulator is a device which monitors system voltage, detects changes, and makes the required adjustments in the output of the alternator to maintain a constant regulated system voltage. It must do this at low RPM, such as during taxi, as well as at high RPM in flight. In a 28-volt system, it will maintain 28 volts ±0.5 volts.

28. Why is the generator/alternator voltage output slightly higher than the battery voltage? (FAA-H-8083-25)

The difference in voltage keeps the battery charged. For example, a 12-volt battery would be supplied with 14 volts.

29. How does the aircraft cabin heat work? (AFM)

Fresh air, heated by an exhaust shroud, is directed to the cabin through a series of ducts.

30. How does the pilot control temperature in the cabin? (AFM)

Temperature is controlled by mixing outside air (cabin air control) with heated air (cabin heat control) in a manifold near the cabin firewall. This air is then ducted to vents located on the cabin floor.

31. What are the two types of oil available for use in your airplane?

Mineral oil—Also known as nondetergent oil. It contains no additives. This type oil is normally used after an engine overhaul or when an aircraft engine is new, for engine break-in purposes.

Ashless dispersant—Mineral oil with additives. It has high antiwear properties along with multi-viscosity (ability to perform in a wide range of temperatures). It also picks up contamination and carbon particles and keeps them suspended so that buildups and sludge do not form in the engine.

B. System and Equipment Malfunctions

1. What causes "carburetor icing," and what are the first indications of its presence? (FAA-H-8083-25)

The vaporization of fuel, combined with the expansion of air as it passes through the carburetor, causes a sudden cooling of the mixture. The temperature of the air passing through the carburetor may drop as much as 60°F within a fraction of a second. Water vapor is squeezed out by this cooling, and if the temperature in the carburetor reaches 32°F or below, the moisture will be deposited as frost or ice inside the carburetor. For airplanes with a fixed-pitch propeller, the first indication of carburetor icing is loss of RPM. For airplanes with controllable-pitch (constant-speed) propellers, the first indication is usually a drop in manifold pressure.

2. What method is used to determine that carburetor ice has been eliminated? (FAA-H-8083-25)

When heat is first applied, there will be a drop in RPM in airplanes equipped with a fixed-pitch propeller; there will be a drop in manifold pressure in airplanes equipped with a controllable-pitch propeller. If ice is present there will be a rise in RPM or manifold pressure after the initial drop (often accompanied by intermittent engine roughness); and then, when the carburetor heat is turned "off," the RPM or manifold pressure will rise to a setting greater than that before application of heat. The engine should run more smoothly after the ice has been removed.

3. What conditions are favorable for carburetor icing? (FAA-H-8083-25)

Carburetor ice is most likely to occur when temperatures are below 70°F (21°C) and the relative humidity is above 80 percent. However, due to the sudden cooling that takes place in the carburetor, icing can occur even with temperatures as high as 100°F (38°C) and humidity as low as 50 percent. This temperature drop can be as much as 60° to 70°F.

4. What is "detonation"? (FAA-H-8083-25)

Detonation is an uncontrolled, explosive ignition of the fuel/air mixture within the cylinder's combustion chamber. It causes excessive temperature and pressure which, if not corrected, can quickly lead to failure of the piston, cylinder, or valves. In less severe cases, detonation causes engine overheating, roughness, or loss of power. Detonation is characterized by high cylinder head temperatures, and is most likely to occur when operating at high power settings.

5. What action should be taken if detonation is suspected? (FAA-H-8083-25)

Corrective action for detonation may be accomplished by adjusting any of the engine controls which will reduce both temperature and pressure of the fuel air charge.

a. Reduce power.

b. Reduce the climb rate for better cooling.

c. Enrich the fuel/air mixture.

d. Open cowl flaps if available.

Also, ensure that the airplane has been serviced with the proper grade of fuel.

6. What is "preignition"? (FAA-H-8083-25)

Pre-ignition occurs when the fuel/air mixture ignites prior to the engine's normal ignition event resulting in reduced engine power and high operating temperatures. Premature burning is usually caused by a residual hot spot in the combustion chamber, often created by a small carbon deposit on a spark plug, a cracked spark plug insulator, or other damage in the cylinder that causes a part to heat sufficiently to ignite the fuel/air charge. As with detonation, pre-ignition may also cause severe engine damage, because the expanding gases exert excessive pressure on the piston while still on its compression stroke.

7. What action should be taken if preignition is suspected? (FAA-H-8083-25)

Corrective actions for preignition include any type of engine operation which would promote cooling such as:

a. Reduce power.

b. Reduce the climb rate for better cooling.

c. Enrich the fuel/air mixture.

d. Open cowl flaps if available.

8. During the before-takeoff runup, you switch the magnetos from the "BOTH" position to the "RIGHT" position and notice there is no RPM drop. What condition does this indicate?

The left P-lead is not grounding, or the engine has been running only on the right magneto because the left magneto has totally failed.

9. Interpret the following ammeter indications.

a. Ammeter indicates a right deflection (positive).

- *After starting*—Power from the battery used for starting is being replenished by the alternator; or, if a full-scale charge is indicated for more than 1 minute, the starter is still engaged and a shutdown is indicated.

- *During flight*—A faulty voltage regulator is causing the alternator to overcharge the battery. Reset the system and if the condition continues, terminate the flight as soon as possible.

b. Ammeter indicates a left deflection (negative).

- *After starting*—It is normal during start. At other times this indicates the alternator is not functioning or an overload condition exists in the system. The battery is not receiving a charge.

- *During flight*—The alternator is not functioning or an overload exists in the system. The battery is not receiving a charge. Possible causes: the master switch was accidentally shut off, or the alternator circuit breaker tripped.

10. What action should be taken if the ammeter indicates a continuous discharge while in flight?

The alternator has quit producing a charge, so the alternator circuit breaker should be checked and reset if necessary. If this does not correct the problem, the following should be accomplished:

a. The alternator should be turned off; pull the circuit breaker (the field circuit will continue to draw power from the battery).

b. All electrical equipment not essential to flight should be turned off (the battery is now the only source of electrical power).

c. The flight should be terminated and a landing made as soon as possible.

11. What action should be taken if the ammeter indicates a continuous charge while in flight (more than two needle widths)?

If a continuous excessive rate of charge were allowed for any extended period of time, the battery would overheat and evaporate the electrolyte at an excessive rate. A possible explosion of the battery could result. Also, electronic components in the electrical system would be adversely affected by higher than normal voltage. Protection is provided by an overvoltage sensor which will shut the alternator down if an excessive voltage is detected. If this should occur the following should be done:

a. The alternator should be turned off; pull the circuit breaker (the field circuit will continue to draw power from the battery).

b. All electrical equipment not essential to flight should be turned off (the battery is now the only source of electrical power).

c. The flight should be terminated and a landing made as soon as possible.

12. During a cross-country flight you notice that the oil pressure is low, but the oil temperature is normal. What is the problem and what action should be taken?

A low oil pressure in flight could be the result of any one of several problems, the most common being that of insufficient oil. If the oil temperature continues to remain normal, a clogged oil pressure relief valve or an oil pressure gauge malfunction could be the culprit. In any case, a landing at the nearest airport is advisable to check for the cause of trouble.

13. What procedures should be followed concerning a partial loss of power in flight? (AFM)

If a partial loss of power occurs, the first priority is to establish and maintain a suitable airspeed (best glide airspeed if necessary). Then, select an emergency landing area and remain within gliding distance. As time allows, attempt to determine the cause and correct it.

Complete the following checklist:

a. Check the carburetor heat.

b. Check the amount of fuel in each tank and switch fuel tanks if necessary.

c. Check the fuel selector valve's current position.

d. Check the mixture control.

e. Check that the primer control is all the way in and locked.

f. Check the operation of the magnetos in all three positions; both, left or right.

14. What procedures should be followed if an engine fire develops in flight? (AFM)

In the event of an engine fire in flight, the following procedures should be used:

a. Set the mixture control to "Idle cutoff."

b. Set the fuel selector valve to "Off."

c. Turn the master switch to "Off."

d. Set the cabin heat and air vents to "Off"; leave the overhead vents "On."

e. Establish an airspeed of 100 KIAS and increase the descent, if necessary, to find an airspeed that will provide for an incombustible mixture.

f. Execute a forced landing procedures checklist.

15. **What procedures should be followed if an engine fire develops on the ground during starting?** (AFM)

Continue to attempt an engine start as a start will cause flames and excess fuel to be sucked back through the carburetor.

a. If the engine starts:
   • Increase the power to a higher RPM for a few moments; and
   • Shut down the engine and inspect it.

b. If the engine does not start:
   • Set the throttle to the "Full" position.
   • Set the mixture control to "Idle cutoff."
   • Continue to try an engine start in an attempt to put out the fire by vacuum.

c. If the fire continues:
   • Turn the ignition switch to "Off."
   • Turn the master switch to "Off."
   • Set the fuel selector to "Off."

In all cases, evacuate the aircraft and obtain a fire extinguisher and/or assistance.

C. Pitot/Static Flight Instruments

1. **What instruments operate off of the pitot/static system?** (FAA-H-8083-15)

Altimeter, Vertical Speed, and Airspeed Indicator.

2. **How does an altimeter work?** (FAA-H-8083-15)

Aneroid wafers expand and contract as atmospheric pressure changes, and through a shaft and gear linkage, rotate pointers on the dial of the instrument.

3. What are the limitations of a pressure altimeter? (FAA-H-8083-15)

Nonstandard pressure and temperature; temperature variations expand or contract the atmosphere and raise or lower pressure levels that the altimeter senses.

On a warm day —The pressure level is higher than on a standard day. The altimeter indicates lower than actual altitude.

On a cold day — The pressure level is lower than on a standard day. The altimeter indicates higher than actual altitude.

Changes in surface pressure also affect pressure levels at altitude.

Higher than standard pressure—The pressure level is higher than on a standard day. The altimeter indicates lower than actual altitude.

Lower than standard pressure—The pressure level is lower than on a standard day. The altimeter indicates higher than actual altitude.

Remember: High to low or hot to cold, look out below!

4. Define and state how you would determine the following altitudes. (FAA-H-8083-25)

Indicated altitude
Pressure altitude
True altitude
Density altitude
Absolute altitude

Absolute altitude—the vertical distance of an aircraft above the terrain.

Indicated altitude—the altitude read directly from the altimeter (uncorrected) after it is set to the current altimeter setting.

Pressure altitude—the altitude when the altimeter setting window is adjusted to 29.92. Pressure altitude is used for computer solutions to determine density altitude, true altitude, true airspeed, etc.

True altitude—the true vertical distance of the aircraft above sea level. Airport, terrain, and obstacle elevations found on aeronautical charts are true altitudes.

Density altitude—pressure altitude corrected for nonstandard temperature variations. Directly related to an aircraft's takeoff, climb, and landing performance.

5. How does the airspeed indicator operate?
(FAA-H-8083-25)

The airspeed indicator is a sensitive, differential pressure gauge which measures the difference between impact pressure from the pitot head and undisturbed atmospheric pressure from the static source. The difference is registered by the airspeed pointer on the face of the instrument.

6. What is the limitation of the airspeed indicator?
(FAA-H-8083-15)

The airspeed indicator is subject to proper flow of air in the pitot/static system.

7. What are the errors of the airspeed indicator?

Position error—Caused by the static ports sensing erroneous static pressure; slipstream flow causes disturbances at the static port preventing actual atmospheric pressure measurement. It varies with airspeed, altitude and configuration, and may be a plus or minus value.

Density error—Changes in altitude and temperature are not compensated for by the instrument.

Compressibility error—Caused by the packing of air into the pitot tube at high airspeeds, resulting in higher than normal indications. It is usually not a factor at slower speeds.

8. What are the different types of aircraft speeds?
(FAA-H-8083-15)

Indicated airspeed (IAS)—read off the instrument.

Calibrated airspeed (CAS)—IAS corrected for instrument and position errors; obtained from the Pilot's Operating Handbook or off the face of the instrument.

Equivalent airspeed (EAS)—CAS corrected for adiabatic compressible flow at altitude.

Continued

True airspeed (TAS)—CAS corrected for nonstandard temperature and pressure; obtained from the flight computer, POH or A/S indicator slide computer.

Ground speed (GS)—TAS corrected for wind; speed across ground; use the flight computer.

9. Name several important airspeed limitations not marked on the face of the airspeed indicator. (FAA-H-8083-25)

Maneuvering speed (V_A)—the "rough air" speed and the maximum speed for abrupt maneuvers. If rough air or severe turbulence is encountered during flight, the airspeed should be reduced to maneuvering speed or less to minimize the stress on the airplane structure.

Landing Gear Operating speed (V_{LO})—the maximum speed for extending or retracting the landing gear if using aircraft equipped with retractable landing gear.

Best Angle-of-Climb speed (V_X)—important when a short-field takeoff to clear an obstacle is required.

Best Rate-of-Climb speed (V_Y)—the airspeed that will give the pilot the most altitude in a given period of time.

10. What airspeed limitations apply to the color-coded marking system of the airspeed indicator? (FAA-H-8083-25)

White Arc .... flap operating range
Lower A/S Limit White Arc .... V_{SO} (stall speed landing configuration)
Upper A/S Limit White Arc .... V_{FE} (maximum flap extension speed)
Green Arc .... normal operating range
Lower A/S Limit Green Arc .... V_{S1} (stall speed clean or specified configuration)
Upper A/S Limit Green Arc .... V_{NO} (normal operations speed or maximum structural cruise speed)
Yellow Arc .... Caution Range (operations in smooth air only)
Red Line .... V_{NE} (maximum speed for operations in smooth air only)

11. How does the vertical speed indicator work?
(FAA-H-8083-15)

The vertical speed indicator is a pressure differential instrument. Inside the instrument case is an aneroid very much like the one in an airspeed indicator. Both the inside of this aneroid and the inside of the instrument case are vented to the static system, but the case is vented through a calibrated orifice that causes the pressure inside the case to change more slowly than the pressure inside the aneroid. As the aircraft ascends, the static pressure becomes lower and the pressure inside the case compresses the aneroid, moving the pointer upward, showing a climb and indicating the number of feet per minute the aircraft is ascending.

12. What are the limitations of the vertical speed indicator?
(FAA-H-8083-25)

The VSI is not accurate until the aircraft is stabilized. Because of the restriction in airflow to the static line, a 6 to 9 second lag is required to equalize or stabilize the pressures. Sudden or abrupt changes in aircraft attitude will cause erroneous instrument readings as airflow fluctuates over the static port. Both rough control technique and turbulent air result in unreliable needle indications.

D. Gyroscopic Flight Instruments

1. What instruments contain gyroscopes? (FAA-H-8083-25)

a. the turn coordinator
b. the heading indicator (directional gyro)
c. the attitude indicator (artificial horizon)

2. What are the two fundamental properties of a gyroscope? (FAA-H-8083-25)

Rigidity in space—a gyroscope remains in a fixed position in the plane in which it is spinning.

Precession—the tilting or turning of a gyro in response to a deflective force. The reaction to this force does not occur at the point where it was applied; rather, it occurs at a point that is 90° later in the direction of rotation. The rate at which the gyro precesses is inversely proportional to the speed of the rotor and proportional to the deflective force.

3. What are the various power sources that may be used to power the gyroscopic instruments in an airplane? (FAA-H-8083-25)

In some airplanes, all the gyros are vacuum, pressure, or electrically operated; in others, vacuum or pressure systems provide the power for the heading and attitude indicators, while the electrical system provides the power for the turn coordinator. Most airplanes have at least two sources of power to ensure at least one source of bank information if one power source fails.

4. How does the vacuum system operate? (FAA-H-8083-25)

An engine-driven vacuum pump provides suction which pulls air from the instrument case. Normal pressure entering the case is directed against rotor vanes to turn the rotor (gyro) at high speed, much like a water wheel or turbine operates. Air is drawn into the instrument through a filter from the cockpit and eventually vented outside. Vacuum values vary between manufacturers (usually between 4.5 and 5.5 in. Hg.), but provide rotor speeds from 8,000 to 18,000 RPM.

5. How does the attitude indicator work? (FAA-H-8083-25)

The gyro in the attitude indicator is mounted on a horizontal plane and depends upon rigidity in space for its operation. The horizon bar represents the true horizon. This bar is fixed to the gyro and remains in a horizontal plane as the airplane is pitched or banked about its lateral or longitudinal axis, indicating the attitude of the airplane relative to the true horizon.

6. What are the limitations of an attitude indicator? (FAA-H-8083-25)

The pitch and bank limits depend upon the make and model of the instrument. Limits in the banking plane are usually from 100 degrees to 110 degrees, and the pitch limits are usually from 60 to 70 degrees. If either limit is exceeded, the instrument will tumble or spill and will give incorrect indications until reset. A number of modern attitude indicators will not tumble.

7. What are the errors of the attitude indicator?
(FAA-H-8083-15)

Attitude indicators are free from most errors, but depending upon the speed with which the erection system functions, there may be a slight nose-up indication during a rapid acceleration and a nose-down indication during a rapid deceleration. There is also a possibility of a small bank angle and pitch error after a 180° turn. These inherent errors are small and correct themselves within a minute or so after returning to straight-and-level flight.

8. How does the heading indicator operate?
(FAA-H-8083-25)

The operation of the heading indicator uses the principle of rigidity in space. The rotor turns in a vertical plane, and the compass card is fixed to the rotor. Since the rotor remains rigid in space, the points on the card hold the same position in space relative to the vertical plane. As the instrument case and the airplane revolve around the vertical axis, the card provides clear and accurate heading information.

9. What are the limitations of the heading indicator?
(FAA-H-8083-25)

The bank and pitch limits of the heading indicator vary with the particular design and make of instrument. On some heading indicators found in light airplanes, the limits are approximately 55 degrees of pitch and 55 degrees of bank. When either of these attitude limits is exceeded, the instrument "tumbles" or "spills" and no longer gives the correct indication until reset. After spilling, it may be reset with the caging knob. Many of the modern instruments used are designed in such a manner that they will not tumble.

10. What error is the heading indicator subject to?
(FAA-H-8083-25)

Because of precession, caused chiefly by friction, the heading indicator will creep or drift from a heading to which it is set. Among other factors, the amount of drift depends largely upon the condition of the instrument. The heading indicator may indicate as much as 15° error per every hour of operation.

11. How does the turn coordinator operate? (FAA-H-8083-15)

The turn part of the instrument uses precession to indicate direction and approximate rate of turn. A gyro reacts by trying to move in reaction to the force applied thus moving the needle or miniature aircraft in proportion to the rate of turn. The slip/skid indicator is a liquid-filled tube with a ball that reacts to centrifugal force and gravity.

12. What information does the turn coordinator provide? (FAA-H-8083-25)

The turn coordinator shows the yaw and roll of the aircraft around the vertical and longitudinal axes.

The miniature airplane will indicate direction of the turn as well as rate of turn. When aligned with the turn index, it represents a standard rate of turn of 3° per second. The inclinometer of the turn coordinator indicates the coordination of aileron and rudder. The ball indicates whether the airplane is in coordinated flight or is in a slip or skid.

13. What will the turn indicator indicate when the aircraft is in a "skidding" or a "slipping" turn? (FAA-H-8083-25)

Slip—The ball in the tube will be on the inside of the turn; not enough rate of turn for the amount of bank.

Skid—The ball in the tube will be to the outside of the turn; too much rate of turn for the amount of bank.

E. Magnetic Compass

1. How does the magnetic compass work? (FAA-H-8083-25)

Magnetized needles fastened to a float assembly, around which is mounted a compass card, align themselves parallel to the earth's lines of magnetic force. The float assembly is housed in a bowl filled with acid-free white kerosene.

2. What limitations does the magnetic compass have? (FAA-H-8083-15)

The float assembly of the compass is balanced on a pivot, which allows free rotation of the card, and allows it to tilt at an angle up to 18 degrees.

3. What are the various compass errors? (FAA-H-8083-15)

Oscillation error—Erratic movement of the compass card caused by turbulence or rough control technique.

Deviation error—Due to electrical and magnetic disturbances in the aircraft.

Variation error—Angular difference between true and magnetic north; reference isogonic lines of variation.

Dip errors:
Acceleration error—On east or west headings, while accelerating, the magnetic compass shows a turn to the north, and when decelerating, it shows a turn to the south.

Remember: ANDS
A ccelerate
N orth
D ecelerate
S outh

Northerly turning error—The compass leads in the south half of a turn, and lags in the north half of a turn.

Remember: UNOS

U ndershoot
N orth
O vershoot
S outh

Additional Study Questions

1. Does the nose wheel turn when the rudder is depressed in flight? (AFM)

2. If the braking system is not functioning, will the parking brake work? (AFM)

3. If the brakes on the left side (pilot) are not functioning, will the brakes on the right side also be inoperative? (AFM)

4. Explain the procedure for starting your airplane with external power. (AFM)

5. You cannot start your airplane due to a low battery, so you request an external start via a ground power cart. What problems might still occur after the engine has started? (AFM)

6. In the event of an electrical system failure, what time duration can you reasonably expect electrical power from the battery? (AFM)

7. What effect would positioning the master switch to the "Off" position have on aircraft systems while in flight? (FAA-H-8083-25)

8. What instruments are affected when the pitot tube freezes? Static port freezes? (FAA-H-8083-25)

9. What is the purpose of the alternate static source? (FAA-H-8083-25)

10. If you set the altimeter from 29.15 to 29.85, what change occurs? (FAA-H-8083-25)

Cross-Country
Flight Planning

5

A. Navigation

1. What are three common ways to navigate?

To navigate successfully, pilots must know their approximate position at all times or be able to determine it whenever they wish. Position may be determined by:

a. Pilotage (by reference to visible landmarks);

b. Dead reckoning (by computing direction and distance from a known position); or

c. Radio navigation (by use of radio aids).

2. What type of aeronautical charts are available for use in VFR navigation? (AIM 9-1-4)

a. *Sectional Charts*—designed for visual navigation of slow to medium speed aircraft. One inch equals 6.86 nautical miles. They are revised semiannually, except most Alaskan charts which are revised annually.

b. *VFR Terminal Area Charts (TAC)*—TACs depict the Class B airspace. While similar to sectional charts, TACs have more detail because the scale is larger. One inch equals 3.43 nautical miles. Charts are revised semiannually, except in Puerto Rico and the Virgin Islands where they are revised annually.

c. *World Aeronautical Charts (WAC)*—WACs cover land areas for navigation by moderate speed aircraft operating at high altitudes. Because of a smaller scale, WACs do not show as much detail as sectionals or TACs, and therefore are not recommended for pilots of low speed, low altitude aircraft. One inch equals 13.7 nautical miles. WACs are revised annually except for a few in Alaska and the Caribbean, which are revised biennially.

d. *VFR Flyway Planning Charts*—This chart is printed on the reverse side of selected TAC charts. The coverage is the same as the associated TAC. They depict flight paths and altitudes recommended for use to bypass high traffic areas.

3. Be capable of locating the following items on a sectional chart:

Abandoned airports

Air Defense Identification Zone (ADIZ)

Airport elevation

Airports with a rotating beacon

Airports with lighting facilities

Airports with services

Alert Area

Approach Control frequencies

ATIS

Class B airspace

Class C airspace

Class D airspace

Class D airspace ceiling

Class E airspace (without operating control tower)

Class E airspace (controlled airspace 700 foot floor)

Class E airspace (controlled airspace 1,200 foot floor)

Class E airspace extensions to Class D airspace

Class G airspace

CTAF

Flight Service Station frequencies

Glider operating area

Hard surfaced runway airports

HIWAS

Isogonic lines

Maximum elevation figures

Military Airports

Military Training Routes

No fixed-wing Special VFR available

Non-hard surfaced runways

Non-directional radio beacons

Non-tower controlled airport

Obstructions above 1,000 feet AGL

Obstructions below 1,000 feet AGL

Parachute Jumping Area
Part-time lighting
Pilot Controlled Lighting
Private airports
Prohibited area
Restricted area
Runway length
Special VFR not authorized
UNICOM frequencies
Victor airways
Visual check points
VORTAC
Warning area
TRSA (Terminal Radar Service Area) if available
TWEB

4. What is an "isogonic line"? (FAA-H-8083-25)

Shown on most aeronautical charts as broken magenta lines, iso-gonic lines connect points of equal magnetic variation. They show the amount and direction of magnetic variation, which from time to time may vary.

5. What is "magnetic variation"? (FAA-H-8083-25)

Variation is the angle between true north and magnetic north. It is expressed as east variation or west variation depending upon whether magnetic north (MN) is to the east or west of true north (TN), respectively.

6. How do you convert a true direction to a magnetic direction? (FAA-H-8083-25)

To convert true course or heading to magnetic course or heading, note the variation shown by the nearest isogonic line. If variation is west, add; if east, subtract.

Remember: East is Least (Subtract)
              West is Best (Add)

7. What are lines of latitude and longitude?
(FAA-H-8083-25)

Circles parallel to the equator (lines running east and west), parallels of latitude, enable us to measure distance in degrees latitude north or south of the equator. Meridians of longitude are drawn from the North Pole to the South Pole and are at right angles to the equator. The "Prime Meridian," which passes through Greenwich, England, is used as the zero line from which measurements are made in degrees east and west to 180°. The 48 conterminous states of the United States lie between 25 degrees and 49 degrees north latitude and between 67 degrees and 125 degrees west longitude.

8. What is "magnetic deviation"? (FAA-H-8083-25)

Because of magnetic influences within the airplane itself (electrical circuits, radios, lights, tools, engine, magnetized metal parts, etc.) the compass needle is frequently deflected from its normal reading. This deflection is called deviation. Deviation is different for each airplane, and also varies for different headings of the same airplane. The deviation value may be found on a deviation card located in the airplane.

9. Name several types of radio aids to air navigation.
(AIM 1-1-2 through 1-1-7, and 1-1-23)

a. NDB (Nondirectional Radio Beacon)

b. VOR (Very High Frequency Omnidirectional Range)

c. VORTAC (VHF Omnidirectional Range/Tactical Air Navigation)

d. DME (Distance Measuring Equipment)

e. RNAV (Area Navigation) includes INS, LORAN, VOR/DME-referenced, and GPS)

10. What is a "VOR" or "VORTAC"? (FAA-H-8083-25)

VORs are VHF radio stations that project radials in all directions (360°) from the station, like spokes from the hub of a wheel. Each of these radials is denoted by its outbound magnetic direction. Almost all VOR stations will also be VORTACs. A VORTAC (VOR-Tactical Air Navigation), provides the standard bearing information of a VOR plus distance information to pilots of airplanes which have distance measuring equipment (DME).

11. Within what frequency range do VORs operate? (FAA-H-8083-25)

Transmitting frequencies of omnirange stations are in the VHF (very high frequency) band between 108 and 117.95 MHz, which are immediately below aviation communication frequencies.

12. What is a VOR "radial"? (FAA-H-8083-25)

A "radial" is defined as a line of magnetic bearing extending from an omnidirectional range (VOR). A VOR projects 360 radials from the station. These radials are always identified by their direction "from" the station. Regardless of heading, an aircraft on the 360° radial will always be located north of the station.

13. How are VOR NAVAIDs classified? (AIM 1-1-8)

Terminal, Low, and High

14. What reception distances can be expected from the various class VORs? (FAA-H-8083-25)

Class	Distance/Altitudes	Miles
T	12,000' and below	25
L	Below 18,000'	40
H	Below 18,000'	40
H	14,500 – 17,999'	100 (conterminous 48 states only)
H	18,000 – FL450	130
H	Above FL450	100

15. What limitations, if any, apply to VOR reception distances? (AIM 1-1-3)

VORs are subject to line-of-sight restrictions, and the range varies proportionally to the altitude of the receiving equipment.

16. What are the different methods for checking the accuracy of VOR receiver equipment? (14 CFR 91.171)

a. VOT check—plus or minus 4°

b. Ground checkpoint—plus or minus 4°

c. Airborne checkpoint—plus or minus 6°

d. Dual VOR check—4° between each other

e. Selected radial over a known ground point—plus or minus 6°

17. What is an "NDB"? (AIM 1-1-2)

A nondirectional beacon; a low- to medium-frequency radio beacon transmits nondirectional signals whereby the pilot of an aircraft properly equipped can determine bearings and "home" or "track" to the station.

18. Within what frequency range do NDBs operate? (AIM 1-1-2)

These facilities normally operate in the frequency band of 190 to 535 kHz (immediately below AM broadcast bands) and transmit a continuous carrier with either 400 or 1020 Hz modulation. All radio beacons, except compass locators, transmit a continuous three-letter identification code.

19. What is "ADF"? (FAA-H-8083-25)

Automatic Direction Finder—Many general aviation-type airplanes are equipped with automatic direction finder (ADF) radio receiving equipment which operate in the low to medium frequency bands. To navigate using the ADF, the pilot tunes the receiving equipment to a ground station known as a Non-Directional Beacon (NDB). The most common use of ADF is that of "homing" by flying the needle to the station.

20. What are some of the advantages/disadvantages when using ADF for navigation? (FAA-H-8083-25)

Advantages: Low cost of equipment and usually very low maintenance; Low or medium frequencies are not affected by line-of-sight; The signals follow the curvature of the earth; therefore, if the aircraft is within range of the station, the signals can be received regardless of altitude.

Disadvantages: Low frequency signals are very susceptible to electrical disturbances, such as lightning, precipitation static, etc.; These disturbances create excessive static, needle deviations, and signal fades; Particularly at night, there may be interference from distant stations.

21. What are the normal usable service ranges for the various class NDBs? (FAA-H-8083-25)

Compass locator .... under 25 watts .... 15 NM

MH .... under 50 watts .... 25 NM

H .... 50 to 1999 watts .... 50 NM*

HH .... 2000 or more watts .... 75 NM

*Service range of individual facilities may be less than 50 miles

22. What is "RNAV"? (AIM Glossary)

Area Navigation (RNAV) provides enhanced navigational capability to the pilot. RNAV equipment can compute the airplane position, actual track and ground speed, and then provide meaningful information relative to a route of flight selected by the pilot. Typical equipment will provide the pilot with distance, time, bearing and crosstrack error relative to the selected "TO" or "active" waypoint and the selected route. Several distinctly different navigational systems with different navigational performance characteristics are capable of providing RNAV functions. Present day RNAV systems include INS, LORAN, VOR/DME, and GPS.

23. What is "DME"? (AIM 1-1-7)

Distance Measuring Equipment (airborne and ground) — used to measure, in nautical miles, the slant range distance of an aircraft from the DME navigational aid. Aircraft equipped with DME are provided with distance and ground speed information when receiving a VORTAC or TACAN facility. DME operates on frequencies in the UHF spectrum between 960 MHz and 1215 MHz.

24. What is "GPS"? (AIM Glossary)

Global Positioning System — a space-based radio positioning, navigation, and time-transfer system. The system provides highly accurate position and velocity information, and precise time, on a continuous global basis to an unlimited number of properly equipped users. The system is unaffected by weather, and provides a worldwide common grid reference system. The GPS concept is predicated upon accurate and continuous knowledge of the spatial position of each satellite in the system with respect to time and distance from a transmitting satellite to the user. The GPS receiver automatically selects appropriate signals from satellites in view and translates these into three-dimensional position, velocity, and time. System accuracy for civil users is normally 100 meters horizontally.

B. Flight Computers and Basic Calculations

1. **Before attempting a cross-country flight, a pilot will need to know how to make common calculations for time, speed, distance, amount of fuel required, as well as basic wind calculations. Solve the following:**

Time, speed and distance problems:

a. **If time equals 25 minutes and distance equals 47 NM, what will speed be?**

b. **If distance equals 84 NM and speed equals 139 knots, what will time be?**

c. **If speed is 85 knots and time is 51 minutes, what will the distance be?**

    a. 113 knots

    b. 36 minutes

    c. 72 NM

Fuel consumption problems:

a. If gallons-per-hour is 9.3 and time is 1 hour, 27 minutes, how many gallons will be consumed?

b. If time is 2 hours, 13 minutes and gallons consumed is 32, what will the gallons-per-hour be?

c. If gallons consumed is 38 and gallons-per-hour is 10.8, what will the time be?

   a. 13.5 gallons

   b. 14.4 GPH

   c. 3 hours, 31 minutes

True airspeed problems:

a. If altitude is 10,000 feet, temperature is 0°C, and IAS is 115, what will the TAS be?

b. If IAS is 103, altitude is 6,000 feet, and the temperature is -10°C, what will the TAS be?

c. If the temperature is 40°F, the IAS is 115, and the altitude is 11,000 feet, what will the TAS be?

   a. 135 TAS

   b. 110 TAS

   c. 139 TAS

Density altitude problems:

a. If pressure altitude is 1,500 feet and the temperature is 35°C, what will the density altitude be?

b. If pressure altitude is 5,000 feet and the temperature is -10°C, what will the density altitude be?

c. If the pressure altitude is 2,000 feet and the temperature is 30°C, what will the density altitude be?

   a. 4,100 feet

   b. 3,100 feet

   c. 4,200 feet

Continued

Conversion problems:

a. **100 nautical miles = _____ statute miles**

b. **12 quarts oil = _____ pounds**

c. **45 gallons fuel = _____ pounds**

d. **80°F = _____ °C**

e. **20 knots = _____ miles per hour**

  a. 115 SM

  b. 22.5 pounds

  c. 270 pounds

  d. 26.6°C

  e. 23 MPH

Ground speed/true heading problems:

a. **If wind direction is 220, wind speed is 030, true course is 146, and TAS is 135, what will ground speed and true heading be?**

b. **If wind direction is 240, wind speed is 025, true course is 283 and TAS is 165, what will ground speed and true heading be?**

c. **If wind direction is 060, wind speed is 030, true course is 036 and TAS is 140, what will ground speed and true heading be?**

  a. Ground speed is 124, true heading is 158.

  b. Ground speed is 146, true heading is 277.

  c. Ground speed is 112, true heading is 041.

2. Flight log example, VFR flight plan:

Careful preflight planning is extremely important. A wise pilot ensures a successful cross-country flight by getting a good preflight briefing, completing a flight log, and filing a flight plan before flight.

a. Get a preflight briefing consisting of the latest or most current weather, airport, and enroute NAVAID information.

b. Draw course lines and mark checkpoints on the chart.

c. Enter checkpoints on the log.

d. Enter NAVAIDs on the log.

e. Enter VOR courses on the log.

f. Enter altitude on the log.

g. Enter the wind (direction/velocity) and temperature on the log.

h. Measure the true course on the chart and enter it on the log.

i. Compute the true airspeed and enter it on the log.

j. Compute the WCA and GS and enter them on the log.

k. Determine variation from chart and enter it on the log.

l. Determine deviation from compass correction card and enter it on the log.

m. Enter compass heading on the log.

n. Measure distances on the chart and enter them on the log.

o. Figure ETE and ETA and enter them on the log.

p. Calculate fuel burn and usage; enter them on the log.

q. Compute weight and balance.

r. Compute takeoff and landing performance.

s. Complete a Flight Plan form.

t. File the Flight Plan with FSS.

3. Diversion to Alternate/Lost Procedures:

a. What actions should be taken if you become disoriented or lost on a cross-country flight?

Condition I: plenty of fuel and weather conditions good.

- Straighten up and fly right. Fly a specific heading in a direction you believe to be correct (or circle, if unsure); don't wander aimlessly.

- If you have been flying a steady compass heading and keeping a relatively accurate navigation log, it's not likely you will have a problem locating your position.

- If several VORs are within reception distance, use them for a cross-bearing to determine position (even a single VOR can be of enormous help in narrowing down your possible position); or, fly to the station—there's no doubt where you are then.

- Use knowledge of your last known position, elapsed time, approximate wind direction and ground speed, to establish how far you may have traveled since your last checkpoint.

- Use this distance as a radius and draw a semicircle ahead of your last known position on chart. For example, you estimate your ground speed at 120 knots. If you have been flying 20 minutes since your last checkpoint, then the no-wind radius of your semicircle is 40 miles projected along the direction of your estimated track.

- If still unsure of your position, loosen up the eyeballs and start some first-class pilotage. Look for something big. Don't concern yourself with the minute or trivial at this point. Often, there will be linear features such as rivers, mountain ranges, or prominent highways and railroads that are easy to identify. You can use them simply as references for orientation purposes and thus find them of great value in fixing your approximate position.

Condition II: low on fuel; weather deteriorating; inadequate experience; darkness imminent; and/or equipment malfunctioning.

Get it on the ground! Most accidents are the product of mistakes which have multiplied over a period of time and getting lost is no exception: don't push your luck. It may well be that in doing so, you have added the final mistake which will add another figure to the accident statistics. If terrain or other conditions make landing impossible at the moment, don't waste time, for it is of the essence: don't search for the perfect field—anything usable will do. Remember, most people on the ground know where they are, and you know that you do not.

b. If it becomes apparent that you cannot locate your position, what action is recommended at this point?

The FAA recommends the use of the "4 Cs":

- *Climb*—The higher altitude allows better communication capability as well as better visual range for identification of landmarks.

- *Communicate*—Use the system. Use 121.5 MHz if no other frequency produces results. It is guarded by FSS's, control towers, military towers, approach control facilities, and Air Route Traffic Control Centers.

- *Confess*—Once communications are established, let them know your problem.

- *Comply*—Follow instructions.

c. What is "DF guidance"? (AIM Glossary)

DF guidance is given to aircraft in distress or to other aircraft that request the service. Headings are provided to the aircraft by facilities equipped with direction finding equipment. Following these headings will lead the aircraft to a predetermined point such as the DF station or an airport. DF guidance for practice is provided when workload permits.

Continued

d. While en route on a cross-country flight, weather has deteriorated and it becomes necessary to divert to an alternate airport. What is the recommended procedure?

- Mark your present position on the chart; write the current time next to your mark.

- Consider the relative distance to all suitable alternates; select the one most appropriate for emergency.

- Determine the magnetic course to the alternate and divert immediately.

- Wind correction, actual distance and estimated time/fuel can then be computed while enroute to alternate.

Note: Use the radial of a nearby VOR or airway that most closely parallels the course to the alternate. Distances can be determined by placing a finger at the appropriate place on a straight edge of a piece of paper and then measuring the approximate distance on the mileage scale at the bottom of the chart.

C. Radio Communications

1. What is the most common type of communication radio equipment installed in general aviation aircraft? How many channels are available? (FAA-H-8083-25)

In general aviation, the most common types of radios are VHF. A VHF radio operates on frequencies between 118.0 and 136.975 MHz and is classified as 720 or 760 depending on the number of channels it can accommodate. The 720 and 760 uses .025 spacing (118.025, 118.050, etc.) with the 720 having a frequency range up to 135.975 and the 760 going up to 136.975.

2. What is the universal VHF "Emergency" frequency? (AIM 6-3-1)

121.5 MHz; this frequency is guarded by military towers, most civil towers, FSS's, and radar facilities.

3. What frequencies are used for ground control? (FAA-H-8083-25)

The majority of ground control frequencies are 121.6 to 121.9 MHz.

4. What is a "CTAF"? (AIM 4-1-9)

A CTAF (Common Traffic Advisory Frequency) is a frequency designated for the purpose of carrying out airport advisory practices while operating to or from an airport without an operating control tower. The CTAF may be a UNICOM, MULTICOM, FSS or TOWER frequency and is identified in appropriate aeronautical publications.

5. What is "UNICOM," and what frequencies are designated for its use? (AIM 4-1-9)

UNICOM is a nongovernment communication facility which may provide airport information at certain airports. Airports other than those with a control tower/FSS on airport will normally use 122.700, 122.725, 122.800, 122.975, 123.000, 123.050, and 123.075 MHz. Airports with a control tower or an FSS on airport will normally use 122.950 MHz.

6. What does "ATIS" mean? (AIM 4-1-13)

Automatic Terminal Information Service (ATIS) is the continuous broadcast of recorded noncontrol information in selected high-activity terminal areas. Its purpose is to improve controller effectiveness and to relieve frequency congestion by automating the repetitive transmission of essential but routine information.

7. If operating into an airport without an operating control tower, FSS or UNICOM, what procedure should be followed? (AIM 4-1-9, Glossary)

Where there is no tower, FSS, or UNICOM station on the airport, use MULTICOM frequency 122.9 for self-announce procedures. MULTICOM is a mobile service not open to public use, used to provide communications essential to conduct the activities being performed by or directed from private aircraft.

8. What frequencies are monitored by most FSS's other than 121.5? (AIM 4-2-14)

FSS's and supplemental weather service locations are allocated frequencies for different functions; for example, 122.0 MHz is assigned as the Enroute Flight Advisory Service frequency at selected FSS's. In addition, certain FSS's provide Local Airport Advisory on 123.6 MHz. Frequencies are listed in the Airport/Facility Directory. If you are in doubt as to what frequency to use, 122.2 MHz is assigned to the majority of FSS's as a common enroute simplex frequency.

9. What is "Local Airport Advisory Service"? (AIM 4-1-9)

Certain FSS's provide Local Airport Advisory service to pilots when an FSS is physically located on an airport which does not have a control tower or where the tower is operated on a part-time basis. The CTAF (usually 123.6) for FSS's which provide this service will be disseminated in appropriate aeronautical publications. A CTAF FSS provides wind direction and velocity, favored or designated runway, altimeter setting, known traffic, notices to airmen, airport taxi routes, airport traffic pattern information, and instrument approach procedures. The information is advisory in nature and does not constitute an ATC clearance.

10. How can a pilot determine what frequency is appropriate for activating his/her VFR flight plan once airborne?

Two ways:

a. Ask the FSS briefer during the preflight weather briefing.

b. Consult the communications section under flight service for the airport of departure in the Airport/Facility Directory.

11. What is the meaning of a heavy-lined blue box surrounding a NAVAID frequency? (Chart Legend)

A heavy-lined blue box surrounding the radio station data indicates that both standard FSS frequencies are available at all altitudes without terrain interference. The standard frequencies are 121.5 and 122.2.

12. Why would a frequency be printed on top of a heavy-lined box? (Chart Legend)

This usually means that this frequency is available in addition to the standard FSS frequencies.

13. What is the meaning of a thin-lined blue box surrounding a NAVAID frequency? (Chart Legend)

A plain box without frequencies on top indicates that there are no standard FSS frequencies available. These NAVAIDs will have a "no voice" symbol (underline under frequency).

14. Why would a frequency be printed on top of a thin-lined blue box? (Chart Legend)

These frequencies are the best frequencies to use in the immediate vicinity of the NAVAID site, and will ensure reception by the controlling FSS at low altitudes without terrain interference. They will normally be followed by an "R" which indicates that the FSS can receive only on that frequency (you transmit on that frequency). The pilot will listen for a response over the NAVAID frequency.

15. How can a pilot determine the availability of HIWAS when looking at a VFR Sectional chart? (FAA-H-8083-25)

Navaids that have HIWAS capability are depicted on sectional charts with an "H" in the upper right corner of the identification box.

16. What meaning does the letter "T" in a solid blue circle appearing in the top right corner of a NAVAID frequency box have? (Chart Legend)

A Transcribed Weather Broadcast is available. A TWEB is a continuous recording of meteorological and aeronautical information that is broadcast on L/MF and VOR facilities for pilots.

D. Federal Aviation Regulations Part 91

1. If an inflight emergency requires immediate action by the pilot, what authority and responsibilities does he/she have? (14 CFR 91.3)

   a. The PIC is directly responsible for, and is the final authority as to, the operation of that aircraft.

   b. In an inflight emergency requiring immediate action, the PIC may deviate from any rule in Part 91 to the extent required to meet that emergency.

   c. Each PIC who deviates from a Part 91 rule shall, upon request from the Administrator, send a written report of that deviation to the Administrator.

2. What restrictions apply to pilots concerning the use of drugs and alcohol? (14 CFR 91.17)

No person may act or attempt to act as a crewmember of a civil aircraft:

   a. within 8 hours after the consumption of any alcoholic beverage;

   b. while under the influence of alcohol;

   c. while using any drug that affects the person's faculties in any way contrary to safety; or

   d. while having .04 percent by weight or more alcohol in the blood.

3. Is it permissible for a pilot to allow a person who is obviously under the influence of intoxicating liquors or drugs to be carried aboard an aircraft? (14 CFR 91.17)

No. Except in an emergency, no pilot of a civil aircraft may allow a person who appears to be intoxicated or who demonstrates by manner or physical indications that the individual is under the influence of drugs (except a medical patient under proper care) to be carried in that aircraft.

4. May portable electronic devices be operated onboard an aircraft? (14 CFR 91.21)

Aircraft operated by a holder of an air carrier operating certificate or an aircraft operating under IFR may not allow operation of electronic devices onboard their aircraft. Exceptions are: portable voice recorders, hearing aids, heart pacemakers, electric shavers, or any other device that the operator of the aircraft has determined will not cause interference with the navigation or communication system of the aircraft on which it is to be used.

5. Under what conditions may objects be dropped from an aircraft? (14 CFR 91.15)

No pilot-in-command of a civil aircraft may allow any object to be dropped from that aircraft in flight that creates a hazard to persons or property. However, this section does not prohibit the dropping of any object if reasonable precautions are taken to avoid injury or damage to persons or property.

6. Concerning a flight in the local area, is any preflight action required, and if so, what must it consist of? (14 CFR 91.103)

Yes, pilots must familiarize themselves with all available information concerning that flight, including runway lengths at airports of intended use, and takeoff and landing distance data under existing conditions.

7. Preflight action as required by regulation for all flights away from the vicinity of the departure airport shall include a review of what specific information? (14 CFR 91.103)

For a flight under IFR or a flight not in the vicinity of an airport:

a. Weather reports and forecasts

b. Fuel requirements

c. Alternatives available if the planned flight cannot be completed

d. Any known traffic delays of which the pilot-in-command has been advised by ATC

e. Runway lengths of intended use

f. Takeoff and landing distance data

8. Which persons on board an aircraft are required to use seatbelts and when? (14 CFR 91.107)

Each person on board a U.S.-registered civil aircraft must occupy an approved seat or berth with a safety belt, and if installed, shoulder harness, properly secured about him or her during movement on the surface, takeoff and landing. However a person who has not reached his or her second birthday and does not occupy or use any restraining device may be held by an adult who is occupying a seat or berth, and a person on board for the purpose of engaging in sport parachuting may use the floor of the aircraft as a seat.

9. What responsibility does the pilot-in-command have concerning passengers and their use of seatbelts? (14 CFR 91.107)

No pilot may take off a U.S. registered civil aircraft unless the pilot-in-command of that aircraft ensures that each person on board is briefed on how to fasten and unfasten that person's safety belt and shoulder harness, if installed. The pilot-in-command shall ensure that all persons on board have been notified to fasten their seatbelt and shoulder harness, if installed, before movement of the aircraft on the surface, takeoff or landing.

10. When are flight crewmembers required to keep their seatbelts and shoulder harnesses fastened? (14 CFR 91.105)

During takeoff and landing, and while en route, each required flight crewmember shall keep his/her seatbelt fastened while at his/her station. During takeoff and landing this includes shoulder harnesses, if installed, unless it interferes with other required duties.

11. **If operating an aircraft in close proximity to another, such as formation flight, what regulations apply?** (14 CFR 91.111)

    a. No person may operate an aircraft so close to another aircraft as to create a collision hazard.

    b. No person may operate an aircraft in formation flight except by arrangement with the pilot-in-command of each aircraft in the formation.

    c. No person may operate an aircraft, carrying passengers for hire, in formation flight.

12. **What is the order of right-of-way as applied to the different categories of aircraft?** (14 CFR 91.113)

    B alloons

    G liders

    A irships

    A irplanes

    R otorcraft

    Aircraft towing or refueling other aircraft have the right-of-way over all other engine-driven aircraft.

    Remember: BGAAR (BIG "R")

13. **When would an aircraft have the right-of-way over all other air traffic?** (14 CFR 91.113)

    An aircraft in distress has the right-of-way over all other air traffic.

14. **State the required action for each of the aircraft confrontations (same category), below.** (14 CFR 91.113)

    Converging

    Approaching head-on

    Overtaking

    Converging: aircraft on right has the right-of-way.

    Approaching head-on: both aircraft shall alter course to right.

    Overtaking: aircraft being overtaken has the right-of-way; pilot of the overtaking aircraft shall alter course to the right.

15. **What right-of-way rules apply when two or more aircraft are approaching an airport for the purpose of landing?** (14 CFR 91.113)

Aircraft on final approach to land or while landing have the right-of-way over aircraft in flight or operating on the surface, except that they shall not take advantage of this rule to force an aircraft off the runway surface which has already landed and is attempting to make way for an aircraft on final approach. When two or more aircraft are approaching an airport for the purpose of landing, the aircraft at the lower altitude has the right-of-way, but it shall not take advantage of this rule to cut in front of another which is on final approach to land or to overtake that aircraft.

16. **Unless otherwise authorized or required by ATC, what is the maximum indicated airspeed at which a person may operate an aircraft below 10,000 feet MSL?** (14 CFR 91.117)

No person may operate an aircraft below 10,000 feet MSL at an indicated airspeed of more than 250 knots (288 MPH).

17. **What is the minimum safe altitude that an aircraft may be operated over a congested area of a city?** (14 CFR 91.119)

Except when necessary for takeoff or landing, no person may operate an aircraft over a congested area of a city, town, or settlement, or over any open-air assembly of persons, below an altitude of 1,000 feet above the highest obstacle within a horizontal radius of 2,000 feet of the aircraft.

18. **In areas other than congested areas, what minimum safe altitudes shall be used?** (14 CFR 91.119)

Except when necessary for takeoff or landing, an aircraft shall be operated no lower than 500 feet above the surface, except over open water or sparsely populated areas. In those cases, the aircraft may not be operated closer than 500 feet to any person, vessel, vehicle or structure.

19. Define "minimum safe altitude." (14 CFR 91.119)

An altitude allowing, if a power unit fails, an emergency landing without undue hazard to persons or property on the surface.

20. What is the lowest altitude an aircraft may be operated over an area designated as a U.S. wildlife refuge, park or Forest Service Area? (AIM 7-4-6)

All aircraft are requested to maintain a minimum altitude of 2,000 feet above the surface.

21. When flying below 18,000 feet MSL, cruising altitude must be maintained by reference to an altimeter set using what procedure? (14 CFR 91.121)

When the barometric pressure is 31.00" Hg or less, each person operating an aircraft shall maintain the cruising altitude or flight level of that aircraft, as the case may be, by reference to an altimeter set to the current reported altimeter setting of a station along the route and within 100 nautical miles of the aircraft. If there is no station within this area, the current reported altimeter setting of an available station may be used. If the barometric pressure exceeds 31.00" Hg, consult the *Aeronautical Information Manual* for correct procedures.

22. If an altimeter setting is not available before flight, what procedure should be used? (14 CFR 91.121)

Use the same procedure as in the case of an aircraft not equipped with a radio: the elevation of the departure airport or an appropriate altimeter setting available before departure should be used.

23. When may a pilot intentionally deviate from an ATC clearance or instruction? (14 CFR 91.123)

No pilot may deviate from an ATC clearance unless:

a. an amended clearance has been obtained,

b. an emergency exists,

c. or in response to a traffic and collision avoidance system resolution advisory.

24. As pilot-in-command, what action, if any, is required of you if you deviate from an ATC instruction and priority is given? (14 CFR 91.123)

Two actions are required of you as PIC:

a. Each pilot-in-command who, in an emergency, deviates from an ATC clearance or instruction shall notify ATC of that deviation as soon as possible (in-the-air responsibility).

b. Each pilot-in-command who is given priority by ATC in an emergency shall submit a detailed report of that emergency within 48 hours to the manager of that ATC facility, if requested by ATC (on-the-ground responsibility).

25. In the event of radio failure while operating an aircraft to, from, through or on an airport having an operational tower, what are the different types and meanings of light gun signals you might receive from an ATC tower? (14 CFR 91.125)

Light	On Ground	In Air
Steady Green	Cleared for Takeoff	Cleared to Land
Flashing Green	Cleared to Taxi	Return for Landing
Steady Red	Stop	Yield, Continue Circling
Flashing Red	Taxi Clear of Runway	Unsafe, Do Not Land
Flashing White	Return to Start	Not Used
Alternate Red/Green	Exercise Extreme Caution	Exercise Extreme Caution

Note: Most pilots find these hard to remember; attach them to your kneeboard or your flight log form.

26. **If the aircraft radio fails in flight under VFR while operating into a tower controlled airport, what conditions must be met before a landing may be made at that airport?** (14 CFR 91.126, 91.127, 91.129)

    a. Weather conditions must be at or above basic VFR weather minimums;

    b. Visual contact with the tower is maintained; and

    c. A clearance to land is received.

27. **What procedures should be used when attempting communications with a tower when the aircraft transmitter or receiver or both are inoperative?** (AIM 4-2-13)

    Arriving Aircraft Receiver Inoperative:

    a. Remain outside or above Class D surface area.

    b. Determine direction and flow of traffic.

    c. Advise tower of aircraft type, position, altitude, and intention to land. Request to be controlled by light signals.

    d. At 3 to 5 miles, advise tower of position and join traffic pattern.

    e. Watch tower for light gun signals.

    Arriving Aircraft Transmitter Inoperative:

    a. Remain outside or above Class D surface area.

    b. Determine direction and flow of traffic.

    c. Monitor frequency for landing or traffic information.

    d. Join the traffic pattern and watch for light gun signals.

    e. Daytime, acknowledge by rocking wings. Nighttime, acknowledge by flashing landing light or navigation lights.

    Arriving Aircraft Transmitter and Receiver Inoperative:

    a. Remain outside or above Class D surface area.

    b. Determine direction and flow of traffic.

    c. Join the traffic pattern and watch for light gun signals.

    d. Acknowledge light signals as noted above.

28. **What general rules apply concerning traffic pattern operations at non-tower airports within Class E or G airspace?** (14 CFR 91.126, 91.127)

Each person operating an aircraft to or from an airport without an operating control tower shall:

a. in the case of an airplane approaching to land, make all turns of that airplane to the left unless the airport displays approved light signals or visual markings indicating that turns should be made to the right, in which case the pilot shall make all turns to the right.

b. in the case of an aircraft departing an airport, comply with any traffic patterns established for that airport in Part 93.

29. **What procedure should be used when approaching to land on a runway with a Visual Approach Slope Indicator?** (14 CFR 91.129)

Aircraft approaching to land on a runway served by a Visual Approach Slope Indicator shall maintain an altitude at or above the glide slope until a lower altitude is necessary for a safe landing.

30. **What is the fuel requirement for VFR flight at night?** (14 CFR 91.151)

No person may begin a flight in an airplane under VFR conditions unless (considering wind and forecast weather conditions) there is enough fuel to fly to the first point of intended landing and, assuming normal cruising speed, at night, to fly after that for at least 45 minutes.

31. **What is the fuel requirement for VFR flight during the day?** (14 CFR 91.151)

During the day, you must be able to fly to the first point of intended landing, and assuming normal cruising speed, to fly after that for at least 30 minutes.

32. When operating an aircraft under VFR in level cruising flight at an altitude of more than 3,000 feet above the surface, what rules apply concerning specific altitudes flown? (14 CFR 91.159)

When operating above 3,000 feet AGL but less than 18,000 feet MSL on a *magnetic course* of 0° to 179°, fly at an odd-thousand-foot MSL altitude plus 500 feet. When on a *magnetic course* of 180° to 359°, fly at an even-thousand-foot MSL altitude plus 500 feet.

33. What instruments and equipment are required for VFR day flight? (14 CFR 91.205)

For VFR flight during the day, the following instruments and equipment are required:

T achometer for each engine
O il pressure gauge for each engine
M anifold pressure gauge for each altitude engine
A ltimeter
T emperature gauge for each liquid-cooled engine
O il temperature gauge for each air-cooled engine

F uel gauge indicating the quantity in each tank
F lotation gear—if operated for hire over water beyond power-off gliding distance from shore
L anding gear position indicator, if the airplane has retractable gear
A irspeed indicator
A nticollision light system—aviation red and white for small air-planes certificated after March 11, 1996
M agnetic direction indicator
E mergency locator transmitter (if required by 14 CFR 91.207)
S afety belts (and shoulder harnesses for each front seat in aircraft manufactured after 1978)

34. What instruments and equipment are required for VFR night flight? (14 CFR 91.205)

For VFR flight at night, all the instruments and equipment for VFR day flight are required, plus the following:

F uses—one spare set or three fuses of each kind required accessible to the pilot in flight

L anding light—if the aircraft is operated for hire

A nticollision light system—approved aviation red or white

P osition lights—(navigation lights)

S ource of electrical energy—adequate for all installed electrical and radio equipment

35. What is an "ELT"? (AIM Glossary)

Emergency Locator Transmitter—A radio transmitter attached to the aircraft structure which operates from its own power source on 121.5 and 243.0 MHz. It aids in locating downed aircraft by radiating a downward-seeping audio tone, 2-4 times a second. It is designed to function without human action after an accident. It can be operationally tested during the first 5 minutes after any hour.

36. Is an emergency locator transmitter required on all aircraft? (14 CFR 91.207)

No person may operate a U.S. registered civil airplane unless there is attached to the airplane an automatic-type emergency locator transmitter that is in operable condition. Several exceptions exist, including the following:

a. Aircraft engaged in training operations conducted entirely within a 50-nautical-mile radius of the airport from which such local flight operations began.

b. Aircraft engaged in design and testing.

c. New aircraft engaged in manufacture, preparation and delivery.

d. Aircraft engaged in agricultural operations.

37. When must the batteries in an emergency locator transmitter be replaced or recharged, if rechargeable? (14 CFR 91.207)

Batteries used in ELTs must be replaced (or recharged, if the batteries are rechargeable):

a. When the transmitter has been in use for more than 1 cumulative hour; or

b. When 50 percent of their useful life (or, rechargeable batteries, 50 percent of their useful life of charge), has expired.

Note: The new expiration date for replacing (or recharging) the battery must be legibly marked on the outside of the transmitter and entered in the aircraft maintenance record. This date indicates 50% of the battery's useful life.

38. What are the regulations concerning use of supplemental oxygen on board an aircraft? (14 CFR 91.211)

a. At cabin pressure altitudes above 12,500 feet MSL up to and including 14,000 feet MSL: for that part of the flight at those altitudes that is more than 30 minutes, the required minimum flight crew must be provided with and use supplemental oxygen.

b. At cabin pressure altitudes above 14,000 feet MSL: for the entire flight time at those altitudes, the required flight crew is provided with and uses supplemental oxygen.

c. At cabin pressure altitudes above 15,000 feet MSL: each occupant is provided with supplemental oxygen.

39. According to regulations, where is aerobatic flight of an aircraft not permitted? (14 CFR 91.303)

No person may operate an aircraft in aerobatic flight:

a. Over any congested area of a city, town, or settlement;

b. Over an open air assembly of persons;

c. Within the lateral boundaries of the surface areas of Class B, Class C, Class D, or Class E airspace designated for an airport;

d. Within 4 nautical miles of the center line of a Federal airway;

e. Below an altitude of 1,500 feet above the surface; or

f. When flight visibility is less than 3 statute miles.

40. Define aerobatic flight. (14 CFR 91.303)

For the purposes of this section, aerobatic flight means an intentional maneuver involving an abrupt change in an aircraft's attitude, an abnormal attitude, or abnormal acceleration, not necessary for normal flight.

41. When are parachutes required on board an aircraft?
(14 CFR 91.307)

a. Unless each occupant of the aircraft is wearing an approved parachute, no pilot of a civil aircraft carrying any person (other than a crewmember) may execute any intentional maneuver that exceeds:

- a bank angle of 60° relative to the horizon; or

- a nose-up or nose-down attitude of 30° relative to the horizon.

b. The above regulation does not apply to:

- flight tests for pilot certification or rating; or

- spins and other flight maneuvers required by the regulations for any certificate or rating when given by a CFI or ATP instructing in accordance with 14 CFR 61.67.

E. Airspace

1. What is Class A airspace? (AIM 3-2-2)

Generally, that airspace from 18,000 feet MSL up to and including FL600, including that airspace overlying the waters within 12 nautical miles of the coast of the 48 contiguous states and Alaska; and designated international airspace beyond 12 nautical miles of the coast of the 48 contiguous states and Alaska within areas of domestic radio navigational signal or ATC radar coverage, and within which domestic procedures are applied.

2. Can a flight under VFR be conducted within Class A airspace? (14 CFR 91.135)

No, unless otherwise authorized by ATC, each person operating an aircraft in Class A airspace must operate that aircraft under instrument flight rules (IFR).

3. What is the minimum pilot certification for operations conducted within Class A airspace? (14 CFR 91.135)

The pilot must be at least a private pilot with an instrument rating.

4. What minimum equipment is required for flight operations within Class A airspace? (14 CFR 91.135)

a. A two-way radio capable of communicating with ATC on the frequency assigned.

b. A Mode C altitude encoding transponder.

c. Equipped with instruments and equipment required for IFR operations.

5. How is Class A airspace depicted on navigational charts? (AIM 3-2-2)

Class A airspace is not specifically charted.

6. What is the definition of Class B airspace? (AIM 3-2-3)

Generally, that airspace from the surface to 10,000 feet MSL surrounding the nation's busiest airports in terms of IFR operations or passenger enplanements. The configuration of each Class B airspace area is individually tailored and consists of a surface area and two or more layers (some Class B airspace areas resemble upside down wedding cakes), and is designated to contain all published instrument procedures once an aircraft enters the airspace.

7. What minimum pilot certification is required to operate an aircraft within Class B airspace? (14 CFR 91.131)

No person may take off or land a civil aircraft at an airport within a Class B airspace area or operate a civil aircraft within a Class B airspace area unless:

a. The pilot-in-command holds at least a private pilot certificate;

b. The pilot-in-command holds a recreational pilot certificate and has met the requirements of 14 CFR 61.101; or for a student pilot seeking a recreational pilot certificate met the requirements of 14 CFR 61.94.

Continued

c. The pilot-in-command holds a sport pilot certificate and has met the requirements of 14 CFR 61.325; or the requirements for a student pilot seeking a recreational pilot certificate in 14 CFR 61.94.

d. The aircraft is operated by a student pilot who has met the requirements of 14 CFR 61.94 or 61.95 of this chapter, as applicable.

Certain Class B airspace areas do not allow pilot operations to be conducted to or from the primary airport, unless the pilot-in-command holds at least a private pilot certificate (example: Dallas/Fort Worth International).

8. What is the minimum equipment required for operations of an aircraft within Class B airspace? (14 CFR 91.131)

a. An operable two-way radio capable of communications with ATC on the appropriate frequencies for that area.

b. A Mode C altitude encoding transponder.

c. If IFR, a VOR receiver is also required.

9. Before operating an aircraft into Class B airspace, what basic requirement must be met? (14 CFR 91.131)

Arriving aircraft must obtain an ATC clearance from the ATC facility having jurisdiction for that area prior to operating an aircraft in that area.

10. What minimum weather conditions are required when conducting VFR flight operations within Class B airspace? (14 CFR 91.155)

VFR flight operations must be conducted clear of clouds with at least 3 statute miles flight visibility.

11. How is Class B airspace depicted on navigational charts? (AIM 3-2-3)

Class B airspace is charted on Sectional Charts, IFR En Route Low Altitude, and Terminal Area Charts. A solid shaded blue line depicts the lateral limits of Class B airspace. Numbers indicate the base and top, i.e. $^{100}/_{25}$, $^{100}/_{SFC}$.

12. **What basic ATC services are provided to all aircraft operating within Class B airspace?** (AIM 3-2-3)

   VFR pilots will be provided sequencing and separation from other aircraft while operating within Class B airspace.

13. **It becomes apparent that wake turbulence may be encountered while ATC is providing sequencing and separation services in Class B airspace. Whose responsibility is it to avoid this turbulence?** (AIM 3-2-3)

   The pilot-in-command is responsible. The services provided by ATC do not relieve pilots of their responsibilities to see and avoid other traffic operating in basic VFR weather conditions, to adjust their operations and flight path as necessary to preclude serious wake turbulence encounters, to maintain appropriate terrain and obstruction clearance, or to remain in weather conditions equal to or better than the minimums required by 14 CFR 91.155.

14. **What is the maximum speed allowed when operating inside Class B airspace, under 10,000 feet and within a Class D surface area?** (14 CFR 91.117)

   Unless otherwise authorized or required by ATC, no person may operate an aircraft at or below 2,500 feet above the surface within 4 nautical miles of the primary airport of a Class C or Class D airspace area at an indicated airspeed of more than 200 knots. This restriction does not apply to operations conducted within a Class B airspace area. Such operations shall comply with the "below 10,000 feet MSL" restriction: "No person shall operate an aircraft below 10,000 feet MSL, at an indicated airspeed of more than 250 knots."

15. **When operating beneath the lateral limits of Class B airspace, or in a VFR corridor designated through Class B airspace, what maximum speed is authorized?** (14 CFR 91.117)

   No person may operate an aircraft in the airspace underlying a Class B airspace area designated for an airport or in a VFR corridor designated through such a Class B airspace area, at an indicated airspeed of more than 200 knots (230 MPH).

16. What is Class C airspace? (AIM 3-2-4)

Generally, that airspace from the surface to 4,000 feet above the airport elevation (charted in MSL) surrounding those airports that have an operational control tower, are serviced by a radar approach control, and that have a certain number of IFR operations or passenger enplanements.

17. What are the basic dimensions of Class C airspace? (AIM 3-2-4)

Although the configuration of each Class C airspace area is individually tailored, the airspace usually consists of a 5 NM radius core surface area that extends from the surface up to 4,000 feet above the airport elevation, and a 10 NM radius shelf area that extends from 1,200 feet to 4,000 feet above the airport elevation. The outer area radius will be 20 NM, with some variations based on site specific requirements. The outer area extends outward from the primary airport and extends from the lower limits of radar/radio coverage up to the ceiling of the approach controls airspace.

18. What minimum pilot certification is required to operate an aircraft within Class C airspace? (AIM 3-2-4)

A student pilot certificate.

19. What minimum equipment is required to operate an aircraft within Class C airspace? (14 CFR 91.130, 91.215)

Unless otherwise authorized by the ATC having jurisdiction over the Class C airspace area, no person may operate an aircraft within a Class C airspace area designated for an airport unless that aircraft is equipped with the following:

a. A two-way radio.

b. Automatic pressure altitude reporting equipment with Mode C capability.

20. **When operating an aircraft through Class C airspace or to an airport within Class C airspace, what basic requirement must be met?** (14 CFR 91.130)

    Each person must establish two-way radio communications with the ATC facilities providing air traffic services prior to entering that airspace and thereafter maintain those communications while within that airspace.

21. **Two-way radio communications must be established prior to entering Class C airspace. Define what is meant by "established" in this context.** (AIM 3-2-4)

    If a controller responds to a radio call with, "(aircraft call sign) standby," radio communications have been established. It is important to understand that if the controller responds to the initial radio call *without* using the aircraft identification, radio communications have *not* been established and the pilot may not enter the Class C airspace.

22. **When departing a satellite airport without an operative control tower located within Class C airspace, what requirement must be met?** (14 CFR 91.130)

    Each person must establish and maintain two-way radio communications with the ATC facilities having jurisdiction over the Class C airspace area as soon as practicable after departing.

23. **What minimum weather conditions are required when conducting VFR flight operations within Class C airspace?** (14 CFR 91.155)

    VFR flight operations within Class C airspace require 3 statute miles flight visibility and cloud clearances of at least 500 feet below, 1,000 feet above and 2,000 feet horizontal to clouds.

24. **How is Class C airspace depicted on navigational charts?** (AIM 3-2-4)

    A solid magenta line is used to depict Class C airspace. Class C airspace is charted on Sectional Charts, IFR En Route Low Altitude, and Terminal Area Charts where appropriate.

25. What type of Air Traffic Control services are provided when operating within Class C airspace? (AIM 3-2-4)

When two-way radio communications and radar contact are established, all participating VFR aircraft are:

a. Sequenced to the primary airport.

b. Provided Class C services within the Class C airspace and the outer area.

c. Provided basic radar services beyond the outer area on a workload permitting basis. This can be terminated by the controller if workload dictates.

26. Describe the various types of terminal radar services available for VFR aircraft. (AIM 4-1-17)

Basic radar service — Safety alerts, traffic advisories, limited radar vectoring (on a workload-permitting basis) and sequencing at locations where procedures have been established for this purpose and/or when covered by a letter of agreement.

TRSA service — radar sequencing and separation service for VFR aircraft in a TRSA.

Class C service — This service provides, in addition to basic radar service, approved separation between IFR and VFR aircraft, and sequencing of VFR arrivals to the primary airport.

Class B service — Provides, in addition to basic radar service, approved separation of aircraft based on IFR, VFR, and/or weight, and sequencing of VFR arrivals to the primary airport(s).

27. Where is Mode C altitude encoding transponder equipment required? (AIM 4-1-19)

a. At or above 10,000 feet MSL over the 48 contiguous states or the District of Columbia, excluding that airspace below 2,500 feet AGL.

b. Within 30 miles of a Class B airspace primary airport, below 10,000 feet MSL

c. Within and above all Class C airspace, up to 10,000 feet MSL;

   d. Within 10 miles of certain designated airports, excluding that airspace which is both outside the Class D surface area and below 1,200 feet AGL.

   e. All aircraft flying into, within, or across the contiguous U.S. ADIZ.

28. What is the maximum speed an aircraft may be operated within Class C airspace? (AIM 3-2-4)

Unless otherwise authorized or required by ATC, no person may operate an aircraft at or below 2,500 feet above the surface within 4 nautical miles of the primary airport of a Class C airspace area at an indicated speed of more than 200 knots (230 MPH).

29. What is Class D airspace? (AIM 3-2-5)

Generally, that airspace from the surface to 2,500 feet above the airport elevation (charted in MSL) surrounding those airports that have an operational control tower. The configuration of each Class D airspace area is individually tailored and when instrument procedures are published, the airspace will normally be designed to contain those procedures.

30. When operating an aircraft through Class D airspace or to an airport within Class D airspace, what requirement must be met? (14 CFR 91.129)

Each person must establish two-way radio communications with the ATC facilities providing air traffic services prior to entering that airspace and thereafter maintain those communications while within that airspace.

31. When departing a satellite airport without an operative control tower located within Class D airspace, what requirement must be met? (14 CFR 91.129)

Each person must establish and maintain two-way radio communications with the ATC facility having jurisdiction over the Class D airspace area as soon as practicable after departing.

32. Is an ATC clearance required if flight operations are conducted through a Class D arrival extension area? (AIM 3-2-5, 3-2-6)

Arrival extensions for instrument approach procedures may be Class D or Class E airspace. As a general rule, if all extensions are 2 miles or less, they remain part of the Class D surface area (blue segmented line). However, if any one extension is greater than 2 miles, then all extensions become Class E. Class E airspace areas that serve as extensions (magenta segmented line) to Class B, Class C, and Class D surface areas, provide controlled airspace to contain standard instrument approach procedures without imposing a communications requirement on pilots operating under VFR.

33. What minimum weather conditions are required when conducting VFR flight operations within Class D airspace? (14 CFR 91.155)

VFR flight operations within Class D airspace require 3 statute miles flight visibility and cloud clearances of at least 500 feet below, 1,000 feet above and 2,000 feet horizontal to clouds.

34. How is Class D airspace depicted on navigational charts? (AIM 3-2-5)

Class D airspace areas are depicted on Sectional and Terminal charts with blue segmented lines, and on IFR Enroute Lows with a boxed [D].

35. What type of Air Traffic Control services are provided when operating within Class D airspace? (AIM 3-2-5, 5-5-8, and 5-5-10)

No separation services are provided to VFR aircraft. When meteorological conditions permit, regardless of the type of flight plan or whether or not under the control of a radar facility, the pilot is responsible to see and avoid other traffic, terrain or obstacles. A controller, on a workload permitting basis, will provide radar traffic information, safety alerts and traffic information for sequencing purposes.

36. **What is the maximum speed an aircraft may be operated within Class D airspace?** (AIM 3-2-5)

Unless otherwise authorized or required by ATC, no person may operate an aircraft at or below 2,500 feet above the surface within 4 nautical miles of the primary airport of a Class D airspace area at an indicated airspeed of more than 200 knots (230 MPH).

37. **When a control tower, located at an airport within Class D airspace, ceases operation for the day, what happens to the lower limit of the controlled airspace?** (AIM 3-2-5)

During the hours the tower is not in operation, Class E surface area rules, or a combination of Class E rules down to 700 feet AGL and Class G rules to the surface, will become applicable. Check the A/FD for specifics.

38. **Will all airports with an operating control tower always have Class D airspace surrounding them?** (AIM 4-3-2)

No; some airports do not have the required weather reporting capability necessary for surface based controlled airspace. The controlled airspace over these airports normally begins at 700 feet or 1,200 feet AGL and can be determined from visual aeronautical charts.

39. **What is the definition of Class E (controlled) airspace?** (AIM 3-2-6)

Generally, if the airspace is not Class A, Class B, Class C, or Class D, and it is controlled airspace, it is Class E airspace.

40. **State several examples of Class E airspace.** (AIM 3-2-6)

a. A surface area designated for an airport and configured to contain all instrument approaches.

b. An extension to a surface area—There are Class E airspace areas that serve as extensions to Class B, Class C, and Class D surface areas designated for an airport. Such airspace provides controlled airspace to contain standard instrument approach procedures without imposing a communications requirement on pilots operating under VFR.

Continued

   c. Airspace used for transition—Class E airspace beginning at either 700 or 1,200 feet AGL used to transition to/from the terminal enroute environment.

   d. En Route Domestic Areas—Class E airspace areas that extend upward from a specified altitude and provide controlled airspace in those areas where there is a requirement to provide IFR en route ATC services but the Federal airway system is inadequate.

   e. Federal Airways—The federal airways are within Class E airspace areas and, unless otherwise specified, extend upward from 1,200 feet to, but not including 18,000 feet MSL. It includes the airspace within parallel boundary lines 4 miles each side of the centerline.

   f. Offshore Airspace areas—Class E airspace that extend upward from a specified altitude to, but not including 18,000 feet MSL. These areas provide controlled airspace beyond 12 miles from the coast of the United States in those areas where there is a requirement to provide IFR en route ATC services.

   g. Unless designated at a lower altitude—Class E airspace begins at 14,500 feet MSL to, but not including 18,000 feet MSL overlying the 48 contiguous states, including the waters within 12 miles from the coast of the 48 contiguous states; the District of Columbia; Alaska, including the waters within 12 miles from the coast of Alaska, and airspace above FL600, excluding specified areas in Alaska.

41. What are the operating rules and pilot/equipment requirements to operate within Class E airspace? (AIM 3-2-6)

   a. Minimum pilot certification—student pilot certificate.

   b. No specific equipment requirements in Class E airspace.

   c. No specific requirements for arrival or through flight in Class E airspace.

42. What basic operational requirement must be met if flight operations are to be conducted into a Class E surface area located at a non-tower airport with a prescribed instrument approach? (AIM 3-2-6)

As long as the weather allows flight operations to be conducted under basic VFR minimums, a flight into or out of the Class E airspace may be made without an ATC clearance. However, if basic VFR minimums cannot be maintained an ATC clearance will be necessary for arrival or departure (Special VFR clearance).

43. Are you required to establish communications with a tower located within Class E airspace? (14 CFR 91.127)

Yes; unless otherwise authorized or required by ATC, no person may operate an aircraft to, from, through, or on an airport having an operational control tower unless two-way communications are maintained between that aircraft and the control tower. Communications must be established prior to 4 nautical miles from the airport, up to and including 2,500 feet AGL.

44. How is Class E airspace depicted on navigational charts? (AIM 3-2-6; 14 CFR 71.71; NACO)

Class E airspace below 14,500 feet MSL is charted on Sectional, Terminal, and IFR Enroute Low Altitude charts. The lateral and vertical limits of all Class E controlled airspace up to but not including 18,000 feet are shown by narrow bands of vignette on Sectional and Terminal Area charts. Controlled airspace floors of 700 feet AGL are defined by a magenta vignette; floors other than 700 feet that abut uncontrolled airspace are defined by a blue vignette; differing floors greater than 700 feet AGL are annotated by a symbol and a number indicating the floor. If the ceiling is less than 18,000 feet MSL, the value (prefixed by the word "ceiling") is shown along the limits of the controlled airspace.

45. How are Class E surface extension areas depicted on navigational charts? (NACO)

Class E airspace areas that serve as extensions to Class B, Class C, and Class D airspace are depicted by a magenta segmented line.

46. What is the definition of Class G airspace? (AIM 3-3-1)

Class G or uncontrolled airspace is that portion of the airspace that has not been designated as Class A, B, C, D, or E airspace.

47. Are you required to establish communications with a tower located within Class G airspace? (14 CFR 91.126)

Yes; unless otherwise authorized or required by ATC, no person may operate an aircraft to, from, through, or on an airport having an operational control tower unless two-way communications are maintained between that aircraft and the control tower. Communications must be established prior to 4 nautical miles from the airport, up to and including 2,500 AGL.

48. What are the vertical limits of Class G airspace? (FAA-H-8083-25)

Class G airspace begins at the surface and continues up to the overlying controlled (Class E) airspace, not to exceed 14,500 feet MSL.

49. What is the minimum cloud clearance and visibility required when conducting flight operations in a traffic pattern at night in Class G airspace? (14 CFR 91.155)

When the visibility is less than 3 statute miles but not less than 1 statute mile during night hours, an airplane may be operated clear of clouds if operated in an airport traffic pattern within one-half mile of the runway.

50. What is the main difference between Class G airspace and Class A, B, C, D, and E airspace?

The main difference which distinguishes Class G airspace from Class A, B, C, D, and E airspace is the flight visibility/cloud clearance requirements necessary to operate within it.

51. What minimum flight visibility and clearance from clouds are required for VFR flight in the following situations? (14 CFR 91.155)

Class C, D, or E Airspace

Less than 10,000 feet MSL:
   Visibility: 3 statute miles.
   Cloud clearance: 500 feet below, 1,000 feet above, 2,000 feet
      horizontal.

At or above 10,000 feet MSL:
   Visibility: 5 statute miles.
   Cloud clearance: 1,000 feet below, 1,000 feet above,
      1 statute mile horizontal.

Class G Airspace

1,200 feet or less above the surface (regardless of MSL altitude):
   Day
      Visibility: 1 statute mile.
      Cloud clearance: clear of clouds

   Night
      Visibility: 3 statute miles
      Cloud clearance: 500 feet below, 1,000 feet above,
         2,000 feet horizontal.

More than 1,200 ft. above the surface but less than 10,000 ft. MSL:
   Day
      Visibility: 1 statute mile
      Cloud clearance: 500 feet below, 1,000 feet above,
         2,000 feet horizontal.

   Night
      Visibility: 3 statute miles
      Cloud clearance: 500 feet below, 1,000 feet above,
         2,000 feet horizontal.

More than 1,200 ft. above the surface and at or above
10,000 ft. MSL:
   Visibility: 5 statute miles
   Cloud clearance: 1,000 feet below, 1,000 feet above,
      1 statute mile horizontal.

52. What are the "basic" VFR weather minimums required for operation of an aircraft into Class B, Class C, Class D, or Class E airspace? (14 CFR 91.155)

No person may operate an aircraft, under VFR, within the lateral boundaries of the surface areas of Class C, Class D, or Class E airspace designated for an airport when the ceiling is less than 1,000 feet and the ground visibility is less than 3 statute miles. If ground visibility is not reported at that airport, unless flight visibility during landing or takeoff, or while operating in the traffic pattern is at least 3 statute miles.

Note: Class B only requires clear of clouds and 3 statute miles visibility.

53. If VFR flight minimums cannot be maintained, can a VFR flight be made into Class B, C, D, or E airspace? (AIM 4-4-5)

No, with one exception. A "Special VFR clearance" may be obtained from the controlling authority prior to entering the Class B, C, D, or E airspace provided the flight can be made clear of clouds with at least one statute mile ground visibility if taking off or landing. If ground visibility is not reported at that airport, the flight visibility must be at least 1 statute mile.

54. Are Special VFR clearances always available to pilots in all classes of airspace? (AIM 4-4-5)

A VFR pilot may request and be given a clearance to enter, leave, or operate within most Class D and Class E surface areas and some Class B and Class C surface areas traffic permitting and providing such flight will not delay IFR operations.

Note: Special VFR operations by fixed wing aircraft are prohibited in some Class B and Class C surface areas due to the volume of IFR traffic. A list of these Class B and Class C surface areas is contained in 14 CFR Part 91. They are also depicted on Sectional Aeronautical Charts.

55. **If it becomes apparent that a special VFR clearance will be necessary, what facility should the pilot contact in order to obtain one?** (AIM 4-4-5)

When a control tower is located within a Class B, Class C, or Class D surface area, requests for clearances should be made to the tower. In a Class E surface area, a clearance may be obtained from the nearest tower, FSS, or center.

56. **Can a "Special VFR clearance" be obtained into or out of Class B, C, D, or E airspace at night?** (AIM 4-4-5)

Special VFR operations by fixed-wing aircraft are prohibited between sunset and sunrise unless the pilot is instrument rated and the aircraft is equipped for IFR flight.

57. **What is a "Prohibited Area"?** (AIM 3-4-2)

Prohibited areas contain certain airspace of defined dimensions identified by an area on the surface of the earth within which the flight of aircraft is prohibited. Such areas are established for security or other reasons associated with the national welfare.

58. **What is a "Restricted Area"?** (AIM 3-4-3)

Restricted areas contain airspace identified by an area on the surface of the earth within which the flight of aircraft, while not wholly prohibited, is subject to restrictions. These areas denote the existence of unusual, often invisible, hazards to aircraft such as artillery firing, aerial gunnery, or guided missiles. Penetration of restricted areas without authorization from the using or controlling agency may be extremely hazardous to the aircraft and its occupants.

59. **Under what conditions, if any, may pilots enter restricted or prohibited areas?** (14 CFR 91.133)

No person may operate an aircraft within a restricted area contrary to the restrictions imposed, or within a prohibited area, unless that person has the permission of the using or controlling agency. Normally *no* operations are permitted within a prohibited area and *prior* permission must always be obtained before operating within a restricted area.

60. What is a "Warning Area"? (AIM 3-4-4)

A warning area is airspace of defined dimensions extending from three nautical miles outward from the coast of the United States, containing activity that may be hazardous to nonparticipating aircraft. The purpose of such an area is to warn nonparticipating pilots of the potential danger. A warning area may be located over domestic or international waters, or both.

61. What is a "MOA"? (AIM 3-4-5)

A Military Operating Area (MOA) consists of airspace of defined vertical and lateral limits established for the purpose of separating certain military training activities from IFR traffic. Pilots operating under VFR should exercise extreme caution while flying within an MOA when military activity is being conducted. The activity status (active/inactive) of MOAs may change frequently. Therefore, pilots should contact any FSS within 100 miles of the area to obtain accurate real-time information concerning the MOA hours of operation. Prior to entering an active MOA, pilots should contact the controlling agency for traffic advisories.

62. What is an "Alert Area"? (AIM 3-4-6)

Alert areas are depicted on aeronautical charts to inform nonparticipating pilots of areas that may contain a high volume of pilot training or an unusual type of aerial activity. Pilots should be particularly alert when flying in these areas. All activity within an Alert Area shall be conducted in accordance with regulations, without waiver, and pilots of participating aircraft as well as pilots transiting the area shall be equally responsible for collision avoidance.

63. What are "Controlled Firing Areas"? (AIM 3-4-7)

Controlled Firing Areas (CFAs) contain activities that, if not conducted in a controlled environment, could be hazardous to nonparticipating aircraft. The distinguishing feature of the CFA, as compared to other special use airspace, is that its activities are suspended immediately when spotter aircraft, radar or ground lookout positions indicate an aircraft might be approaching the area. CFAs are not charted.

64. What is a "National Security Area"? (AIM 3-5-7)

National Security Areas consist of airspace of defined vertical and lateral dimensions established at locations where there is a requirement for increased security and safety of ground facilities. Pilots are requested to voluntarily avoid flying through the depicted NSA. When is it necessary to provide a greater level of security and safety, flight in NSAs may be temporarily prohibited by regulation under the provisions of 14 CFR 99.7.

65. Where can information on special use airspace be found? (AIM 3-4-1)

Special use airspace (except CFAs) are charted on IFR or visual charts and include the hours of operation, altitudes, and the controlling agency.

66. Where can a pilot find information on VFR flyways, VFR Corridors, Class B airspace transition routes, and Terminal Area VFR routes used to transition busy terminal airspace? (AIM 3-5-5)

Information will normally be depicted on the reverse side of VFR Terminal Area Charts, commonly referred to as Class B airspace charts.

67. What is an "Airport Advisory Area"? (AIM 3-5-1)

An airport advisory area is the area within 10 statute miles of an airport where a control tower is not operating but where a FSS is located. At such locations, the FSS provides advisory service to arriving aircraft. It is not mandatory that pilots participate in the Airport Advisory program, but it is strongly recommended they do so.

68. What are "Military Training Routes"? (AIM 3-5-2)

Military Training Routes are developed for use by the military for the purpose of conducting low-altitude, high speed training. The routes above 1,500 feet AGL are developed to be flown, to the maximum extent possible, under IFR. The routes at 1,500 feet AGL and below are generally developed to be flown under VFR. Routes below 1,500 feet AGL use four-digit identifiers (i.e. IR 1004, VR 1008). Routes above 1,500 feet AGL use three-digit identifiers, (i.e. IR 003, VR 004). IR is for IFR routes and VR is for VFR routes.

69. What is a "TRSA"? (AIM Glossary)

A Terminal Radar Service Area (TRSA) consists of airspace surrounding designated airports wherein ATC provides radar vectoring, sequencing, and separation on a full time basis for all IFR and participating VFR aircraft. Pilot participation is urged but not mandatory.

70. What class of airspace is a "TRSA"? (AIM 3-5-6)

TRSAs do not fit into any of the U.S. airspace classes and are not contained in 14 CFR Part 71 nor are there any operating rules in Part 91. The primary airport(s) within the TRSA become Class D airspace. The remaining portion of a TRSA overlies other controlled airspace which is normally Class E airspace beginning at 700 or 1,200 feet and established to transition to/from the enroute/terminal environment. TRSAs will continue to be an airspace area where participating pilots can receive additional radar services which have been redefined as TRSA service.

71. How are TRSAs depicted on navigational charts? (AIM 3-5-6)

TRSAs are depicted on VFR sectional and terminal area charts with a solid black line and altitudes for each segment. The Class D portion is charted with a blue segmented line.

72. What is an "ADIZ"? (AIM 5-6-1)

All aircraft entering domestic U.S. airspace from points outside must provide for identification prior to entry. To facilitate early identification of all aircraft in the vicinity of U.S. and international airspace boundaries, Air Defense Identification Zones (ADIZ) have been established.

73. What requirements must be satisfied prior to operations into, within or across an ADIZ? (AIM 5-6-1)

Operational requirements for aircraft operations associated with an ADIZ are as follows:

Flight plan — An IFR or DVFR flight plan must be filed with the appropriate aeronautical facility.

Two-way radio — An operating two-way radio is required.

Transponder—Aircraft must be equipped with an operable radar beacon transponder having altitude reporting (Mode C) capabilities. The transponder must be turned on and set to the assigned ATC code.

Position reports—For IFR flights, normal position reporting. For DVFR flights, an estimated time of ADIZ penetration must be filed at least 15 minutes prior to entry.

Aircraft position tolerances—Over land, a tolerance of ±5 minutes from the estimated time over a reporting point and within 10 NM from the centerline of an intended track over an estimated reporting point. Over water, a tolerance of ±5 minutes from the estimated time over a reporting point or point of penetration and within 20 NM from centerline of an intended track over an estimated reporting point.

F. Airspace Classification Summary

The following section summarizes the requirements for operations within the various airspace classes.

1. Discuss "Class A" airspace.

Vertical dimensions: .... 18,000 ft MSL up to and include FL600

Operations permitted: .... IFR

Entry prerequisites: .... ATC Clearance

Minimum pilot qualifications: .... Instrument rating

Two-way radio communications: .... Yes

VFR minimum visibility: .... N/A

VFR minimum distance from clouds: .... N/A

Aircraft separation: .... All

Conflict resolution: .... N/A

Traffic advisories: .... N/A

Safety advisories: .... Yes

Continued

2. Discuss "Class B" airspace.

Vertical dimensions: .... Surface to 10,000 ft MSL
Operations permitted: .... IFR and VFR
Entry prerequisites: .... ATC clearance
Minimum pilot qualifications: .... Private/Student
Two-way radio communications: .... Yes
VFR Minimum visibility: .... 3 statute miles
VFR Minimum distance from clouds: .... Clear of clouds
Aircraft separation: .... All
Conflict resolution: .... Yes
Traffic advisories: .... Yes
Safety advisories: .... Yes

3. Discuss "Class C" airspace.

Vertical dimensions: .... Surface to 4,000 ft AGL (charted MSL)
Operations permitted: .... IFR and VFR
Entry prerequisites: ... ATC clearance for IFR; radio contact for all
Minimum pilot qualifications: .... Student certificate
Two-way radio communications: .... Yes
VFR Minimum visibility: .... 3 statute miles
VFR Minimum distance from clouds: ..... 500' below, 1,000' above,
and 2,000' horizontal
Aircraft separation: .... IFR, SVFR and runway operations
Conflict resolution: .... Between IFR and VFR operations
Traffic advisories: .... Yes
Safety advisories: .... Yes

4. Discuss "Class D" airspace.

Vertical dimensions: .... Surface to 2,500 ft AGL (charted MSL)
Operations permitted: .... IFR and VFR
Entry prerequisites: ... ATC clearance for IFR; radio contact for all
Minimum pilot qualifications: .... Student certificate
Two-way radio communications: .... Yes
VFR Minimum visibility: .... 3 statute miles
VFR Minimum distance from clouds: ..... 500' below, 1,000' above,
and 2,000' horizontal
Aircraft separation: .... IFR, SVFR and runway operations
Conflict resolution: .... No
Traffic advisories: .... Workload permitting
Safety advisories: .... Yes

5. Discuss "Class E" airspace.

Vertical dimensions: Except for 18,000 feet MSL, no defined vertical limit. Extends upward from either the surface or a designated altitude to the overlying or adjacent controlled airspace.

Operations permitted: ....IFR and VFR
Entry prerequisites: .... ATC clearance for IFR
Minimum pilot qualifications: .... Student certificate
Two-way radio communications: .... Yes for IFR
VFR minimum visibility: .... *3 statute miles
VFR minimum distance from clouds: .... *500' below,
1,000' above, and 2,000' horizontal
Aircraft separation: .... IFR and SVFR
Conflict resolution: ....No
Traffic advisories: .... Workload permitting
Safety advisories: .... Yes

Different visibility minima and distance cloud requirements exist for operations above 10,000 feet MSL and Special VFR.

6. Discuss "Class G" airspace.

Vertical dimensions: .... Surface up to the overlying
controlled (Class E) airspace,
not to exceed 14,500 feet MSL
Operations permitted: ....IFR and VFR
Entry prerequisites: .... None
Minimum pilot qualifications: .... Student certificate
Two-way radio communications: ....No
VFR minimum visibility: .... *1 statute mile
VFR minimum distance from clouds: ... *500' below, 1,000' above,
and 2,000' horizontal
Aircraft separation: .... None
Conflict resolution: ....No
Traffic advisories: .... Workload permitting
Safety advisories: .... Yes

Different visibility minima and distance from cloud requirements exist for night operations, operations above 10,000 feet MSL, and operations below 1,200 feet AGL.

G. National Transportation Safety Board

1. When is immediate notification to the NTSB required? (NTSB Part 830.5)

The operator of an aircraft shall immediately, and by the most expeditious means available, notify the nearest NTSB field office when an aircraft accident or any of the following listed incidents occur:

a. Flight control system malfunction

b. Crewmember unable to perform normal duties

c. Turbine engine failure of structural components

d. Inflight fire

e. Aircraft collision inflight

f. Property damage, other than aircraft, estimated to exceed $25,000

g. Overdue aircraft (believed to be in accident)

2. Define "aircraft incident." (NTSB Part 830.2)

An aircraft incident means an occurrence other than an accident associated with the operation of an aircraft, which affects or could affect the safety of operations.

3. Define "aircraft accident." (NTSB Part 830.2)

An aircraft accident means an occurrence associated with the operation of an aircraft which takes place between the time any person boards the aircraft with the intention of flight and all such persons have disembarked, and in which any person suffers death or serious injury, or in which the aircraft receives substantial damage.

4. Define the term "serious injury." (NTSB Part 830.2)

Serious injury means any injury that:

a. Requires hospitalization for more than 48 hours, commencing within 7 days from the date the injury was received;

b. Results in a fracture of any bone (except simple fractures of fingers, toes or nose);

c. Causes severe hemorrhages, nerve, muscle or tendon damage;

d. Involves any internal organ; or

e. Involves second- or third-degree burns affecting more than 5% of the body surface.

5. Define the term "substantial damage." (NTSB Part 830.2)

"Substantial damage" means damage or failure which adversely affects the structural strength, performance or flight characteristics of the aircraft and which would normally require major repair or replacement of the affected component. Engine failure or damage limited to an engine if only one engine fails or is damaged; bent fairings or cowling; dented skin; small punctured holes in the skin or fabric; ground damage to rotor or propeller blades; and damage to landing gear, wheels, tires, flaps, engine accessories, brakes, or wing tips are not considered substantial damage for the purpose of this part.

6. Will notification to the NTSB always be necessary in any aircraft "accident" even if there were no injuries? (NTSB Part 830)

Refer to the definition of "Accident." An aircraft accident can involve substantial damage and/or injuries, and the NTSB always requires a report if this is the case.

7. Where are accident or incident reports filed? (NTSB Part 830)

The operator of an aircraft shall file any report with the field office of the Board nearest the accident or incident. The National Transportation Safety Board field offices are listed in the U.S. government pages of telephone directories in major cities.

8. After an accident or incident has occurred, how soon must a report be filed with the NTSB? (NTSB Part 830)

The operator shall file a report on NTSB Form 6120.1/2, available from NTSB field offices, the NTSB in Washington D.C., or the FAA Flight Standards District Office:

a. Within 10 days after an accident;

b. When, after 7 days, an overdue aircraft is still missing.

Note: A report on an "Incident" for which notification is required as described shall be filed only as requested by an authorized representative of the NTSB.

9. Can the FAA use reports submitted to NASA for enforcement purposes? (14 CFR 91.25)

The FAA will not use reports submitted to NASA under the Aviation Safety Reporting Program (or information derived therefrom) in any enforcement action except information concerning accidents or criminal offenses which are wholly excluded from the program. By submitting a report within 10 days following an incident, the pilot is not protected from the FAA finding a violation of regulation, but may be providing himself some immunity from a civil penalty or possible suspension of certificate.

H. Aeronautical Information Manual

1. What type of aeronautical lighting is "VASI"? (AIM 2-1-2)

Visual Approach Slope Indicator (VASI) is a system of lights so arranged to provide visual descent guidance information during the approach to a runway. The basic principle of VASI is that of color differential between red and white: each light projects a beam of light having a white segment in the upper half and a red segment in the lower part of the beam. The lights in a two-bar VASI will be as follows:

Red Over Red—below Glide Path

Red Over White—on Glide Path

White Over White—above Glide Path

2. What is "PAPI"? (AIM 2-1-2)

The Precision Approach Path Indicator (PAPI) uses light units similar to the VASI, but are installed in a single row of either two- or four-light units. These systems have an effective visual range of about 5 miles during the day and up to 20 miles at night. The row of light units are normally installed on the left side of the runway.

Four white lights .... High (More than 3.5 degrees)

Three white one red .... Slightly high (3.2 degrees)

Two white two red .... On glide path (3 degrees)

One white three red .... Slightly low (2.8 degrees)

Four red lights .... Low (Less than 2.5 degrees)

3. What does the operation of an airport rotating beacon during the hours of daylight indicate? (AIM 2-1-8)

In Class B, Class C, Class D, and Class E surface areas, operation of the airport beacon during the hours of daylight often indicates that the ground visibility is less than 3 miles and/or the ceiling is less than 1,000 feet. ATC clearance in accordance with 14 CFR Part 91 is required for landing, takeoff and flight in the traffic pattern. Pilots should not rely solely on the operation of the airport beacon to indicate if weather conditions are IFR or VFR. There is no regulatory requirement for daylight operation and it is the pilot's responsibility to comply with proper preflight planning as required by 14 CFR Part 91.

4. What are the six types of signs installed at airports? (FAA-H-8083-25)

a. *Mandatory instruction sign* — red background/white inscription; denotes an entrance to a runway, a critical area, or a prohibited area.

b. *Location sign* — black background/yellow inscription/yellow border; do not have arrows; used to identify a taxiway or runway location, the boundary of the runway, or identify an ILS critical area.

c. *Direction sign* — yellow background/black inscription; identifies the designation of the intersecting taxiway(s) leading out of an intersection that a pilot would expect to turn onto or hold short of.

d. *Destination sign* — yellow background/black inscription and also contain arrows; provides information on locating runways, terminals, cargo areas, and civil aviation areas, etc.

e. *Information sign* — yellow background/black inscription; used to provide the pilot with information on areas that can't be seen from the control tower, applicable radio frequencies, and noise abatement procedures, etc.

f. *Runway distance remaining sign* — black background/white numeral inscription; indicates the distance of the remaining runway in thousands of feet.

5. What color are runway markings? Taxiway markings? (AIM 2-3-2)

Markings for runways are white. Markings for taxiways, areas not intended for use by aircraft (closed and hazardous areas), and holding positions (even if they are on a runway) are yellow.

6. What airport marking aids will be used to indicate the following? (AIM 2-3-2 through 2-3-6)

Runway Threshold Markings—These come in two configurations. They either consist of eight longitudinal stripes of uniform dimensions disposed symmetrically about the runway centerline, or the number of stripes is related to the runway width. A threshold marking helps identify the beginning of the runway available for landing.

Displaced Threshold—A threshold located at a point on the runway other than the designated beginning of the runway. A displaced threshold reduces the length of runway available for landings. The portion of runway behind a displaced threshold is available for takeoffs in either direction. A ten-foot wide white threshold bar is located across the width of the runway at the displaced threshold. White arrows are located along the centerline in the area between the beginning of the runway and displaced threshold. White arrowheads are located across the width of the runway just prior to the threshold bar.

Runway Hold Position Markings—For taxiways, these markings indicate where an aircraft is supposed to stop when it does not have clearance to proceed onto the runway. They are also installed on runways only if the runway is normally used by air traffic control for "land, hold short" operations. They consist of four yellow lines, two solid and two dashed, spaced six inches apart and extending across the width of the taxiway or runway.

Temporarily closed runways and taxiways—Provides a visual indication to pilots that a runway/taxiway is temporarily closed. Yellow crosses are placed on the runway only at each end of the runway. Closed taxiways are blocked with barricades or may utilize a yellow cross at the entrance to the taxiway.

Permanently closed runways and taxiways—For runways and taxiways which are permanently closed, the lighting circuits will be disconnected. The runway threshold, runway designation, and touchdown markings are obliterated and yellow crosses are placed at each end of the runway and at 1,000-foot intervals.

7. **What are the different methods a pilot may use to determine the proper runway and traffic pattern in use at an airport without an operating control tower?** (AIM 4-1-9, 4-3-3)

a. At an airport with a full- or part-time FSS or a full- or part-time UNICOM in operation, an advisory may be obtained which will usually include wind direction and velocity, favored or designated runway, right or left traffic, altimeter setting, known traffic, NOTAMs, etc.

b. At those airports where these services are not available, a segmented circle visual indicator system, if installed, is designated to provide traffic pattern information. The segmented circle system consists of the following components:

   • The segmented circle
   • The wind direction indicator (wind sock, cone, or tee)
   • The landing direction indicator (a tetrahedron)
   • Landing strip indicators
   • Traffic pattern indicators

8. **What is the standard direction of turns when approaching an uncontrolled airport for landing?** (AIM 4-3-3)

When approaching for landing, all turns must be made to the left unless a traffic pattern indicator indicates that turns should be made to the right.

9. **What is considered standard for traffic pattern altitude?** (AIM 4-3-4)

Unless otherwise established, 1,000 feet AGL is the recommended traffic pattern altitude. At most airports and military air bases, traffic pattern altitudes for propeller-driven aircraft generally extend from 600 feet to as high as 1,500 feet AGL. Also, traffic pattern altitudes for military turbojet aircraft sometimes extend up to 2,500 feet AGL.

10. What recommended entry and departure procedures should be used at airports without an operating control tower? (AIM 4-3-3)

A pilot should plan to enter the traffic pattern in level flight, abeam the midpoint of the runway at pattern altitude. When departing a traffic pattern, continue straight out, or exit with a 45-degree turn (to the left when in a left-hand traffic pattern; to the right when in a right-hand traffic pattern) beyond the departure end of the runway, after reaching pattern altitude.

11. If in doubt about the traffic pattern altitude for a particular airport, what publication can provide this information?

The Airport/Facility Directory.

12. What is an "ARTCC," and what useful service can it provide to VFR flights? (AIM Glossary)

An "Air Route Traffic Control Center" is a facility established to provide air traffic control service primarily to aircraft operating on IFR flight plans within controlled airspace and principally during the en route phase of flight. Air Route Surveillance Radar allows them the capability to detect and display an aircraft's position while en route between terminal areas. When equipment capabilities and controller workload permit, certain advisory/assistance service may be provided to VFR aircraft (VFR Flight Following). Frequencies may be obtained from the local FSS or the Airport/Facility Directory.

13. What are the following transponder codes? (AIM 4-1-19, 6-4-2)

1200—VFR operations

7500—Hijack

7600—Communications failure

7700—Emergency

14. When conducting flight operations into an airport with an operating control tower, when should initial contact be established? (AIM 4-3-2)

When operating at an airport where traffic control is being exercised by a control tower, pilots are required to maintain two-way radio contact with the tower while operating within Class B, Class C, and Class D surface areas, unless the tower authorizes otherwise. Initial call-up should be made about 15 miles from the airport. Also, not all airports with an operating control tower will have Class D airspace. These airports do not have weather reporting, which is a requirement for surface-based controlled airspace. Pilots are expected to use good operating practices and communicate with the control tower.

15. What communication procedures are recommended when departing a Class D airspace area? (AIM 4-3-2)

Unless there is good reason to leave the tower frequency before exiting the Class B, Class C and Class D surface areas, it is good operating practice to remain on the tower frequency for the purpose of receiving traffic information. In the interest of reducing tower frequency congestion, pilots are reminded that it is not necessary to request permission to leave the tower frequency once outside of Class B, Class C, and Class D surface areas.

16. How do you convert from standard time to coordinated universal time? (AIM 4-2-12)

You should take the local time (converted to military time) and add the time differential to convert to UTC.

Eastern Standard Time .... add 5 hours

Central Standard Time .... add 6 hours

Mountain Standard Time .... add 7 hours

Pacific Standard Time .... add 8 hours

Alaska Standard Time .... add 9 hours

Hawaii Standard Time .... add 10 hours

Note: For Daylight Savings Time subtract 1 hour from above.

17. **Arrange the radio facilities listed below in the order they would be used when operating into or out of a tower controlled airport within Class B, C, or D airspace.**

    Approach Control

    ATIS

    Ground Control

    Control Tower

    Clearance Delivery

    Departure Control

    Arriving Aircraft: ATIS, Approach Control, Control Tower, Ground Control

    Departing Aircraft: ATIS, Clearance Delivery (if required for the surrounding airspace, i.e., Class B, C or D airspace), Ground Control, Control Tower, Departure Control.

18. **If instructed by ground control to "taxi to" the active runway, can you taxi across a runway if necessary?** (AIM 4-3-18)

    When ATC clears an aircraft to "taxi to" an assigned takeoff runway, the absence of holding instructions authorizes the aircraft to "cross" all runways and taxiways which the taxi route intersects except the assigned takeoff runway.

19. **What are "NOTAMs"?** (AIM 5-1-3)

    Notices To Airmen (NOTAM)—time-critical aeronautical information of either a temporary nature, or not known sufficiently in advance to permit publication on aeronautical charts or in other operational publications, receives immediate dissemination via the National NOTAM System. This is aeronautical information that could affect a pilot's decision to make a flight. It includes such information as airport or primary runway closures, changes in the status of navigational aids, ILS's, radar service availability, and other information essential to planned en route, terminal, or landing operations.

20. What are the three categories of NOTAMs? (AIM 5-1-3)

There are three types of NOTAMs generated by the FAA:

a. *NOTAM (D)*—A NOTAM given (in addition to local dissemination) distant dissemination beyond the area of responsibility of the Flight Service Station. These NOTAMs will be stored and available until canceled. NOTAM Ds contain information on all civil public use airports and navigational facilities that are part of the National Airspace System, and are serious enough to affect whether or not an airport or a certain facility is usable.

b. *NOTAM (L)*—A NOTAM given local dissemination by voice and other means to satisfy local user requirements. It includes such data as taxiway closures, personnel and equipment near or crossing runways, and airport lighting aids that do not affect instrument approach criteria, such as VASI.

c. *FDC NOTAM*—The National Flight Data Center will issue these NOTAMs when it becomes necessary to disseminate information that is regulatory in nature, and they contain such things as amendments to published IAPs and other current aeronautical charts. They are also used to advertise temporary flight restrictions caused by such things as natural disasters or large scale public events that may generate congestion of air traffic over a site.

21. What particular types of NOTAMs will be omitted in a pilot briefing if not specifically requested by the pilot? (AIM 7-1-4)

NOTAM (D) information and FDC NOTAMs published in the Notices to Airmen Publication (NTAP) are not included in pilot briefings unless the pilot specifically requests it. Also, NOTAM (L) information is distributed locally only and is not attached to the hourly weather reports. A separate file of local NOTAMs is maintained at each FSS for facilities in their area only. NOTAM (L) information for other FSS areas must be specifically requested directly from the FSS responsible for the airport concerned.

22. What is the purpose for establishing a temporary flight restrictions (TFR) area? (14 CFR 91.145; AIM 3-5-3)

The FAA will issue a NOTAM designating an area in which a temporary flight restriction (TFR) applies when it determines that this is necessary to protect persons or property on the surface or in the air, to maintain air safety and efficiency, or to prevent the unsafe congestion of aircraft in the vicinity of an aerial demonstration or major sporting event. Always check for appropriate NOTAMs during flight planning.

23. Where can NOTAM information be obtained? (AIM 5-1-3)

a. Nearest FSS

b. DUATs vendors

c. Locally broadcast ATIS

d. Notice to Airman Publication (NTAP)—printed NOTAMs, not normally provided in a briefing; must make a specific request for.

24. When are VFR flight plans required to be filed? (AIM 5-1-4)

Except for operations in or penetrating a Coastal or Domestic ADIZ or DEWIZ, a flight plan is not required for VFR flight; however, it is strongly recommended that one be filed with an FAA FSS when making extended cross-country flights. This will ensure that you receive VFR Search and Rescue Protection.

25. What is a DVFR flight plan? (AIM 5-1-5)

Defense VFR; VFR flights into a Coastal or Domestic ADIZ/DEWIZ are required to file VFR flight plans for security purposes. The flight plan must be filed before departure.

26. When you land at an airport with an ATC tower in operation will the tower automatically close your flight plan? (AIM 5-1-12)

Control towers do not automatically close VFR or DVFR flight plans since they do not know if a particular VFR aircraft is on a flight plan. A pilot is responsible for ensuring that his/her VFR or DVFR flight plan is canceled. You should close your flight plan with the nearest FSS, or if one is not available, you may request any ATC facility to relay your cancellation.

27. If your flight is behind schedule, and you do not report the delay, or you forget to close your flight plan, how much time from ETA does the FSS allow before search and rescue efforts are begun? (AIM 5-1-12)

If you fail to report or cancel your flight plan within one-half hour after your ETA, Search and Rescue procedures are started.

28. What is wake turbulence? (AIM Glossary)

A phenomenon resulting from the passage of an aircraft through the atmosphere. The term includes vortices, thrust stream turbulence, jet blast, jet wash, propeller wash, and rotor wash, both on the ground and in the air.

29. Where are wake turbulence and wingtip vortices likely to occur? (AIM 7-3-3)

All aircraft generate turbulence and associated wingtip vortices. In general, avoid the area behind and below the generating aircraft, especially at low altitudes. Also of concern is the weight, speed, and shape of the wing of the generating aircraft. The greatest vortex strength occurs when the generating aircraft is HEAVY, CLEAN and SLOW.

30. What operational procedures should be followed when wake vortices are suspected to exist? (AIM 7-3-6)

a. *Landing behind a larger aircraft on the same runway:* Stay at or above the larger aircraft's final approach flight path. Note its touchdown point and land beyond it.

b. *Landing behind a larger aircraft, when parallel runway is closer than 2,500 feet:* Consider possible drift to your runway. Stay at or above the larger aircraft's final approach flight path, and note its touchdown point.

c. *Landing behind a larger aircraft, crossing runway:* Cross above the larger aircraft's flight path.

d. *Landing behind a departing larger aircraft on the same runway:* Note the larger aircraft's rotation point, and land well prior to rotation point.

e. *Landing behind a departing larger aircraft, crossing runway:* Note the larger aircraft's rotation point. If past the intersection, continue the approach, and land prior to the intersection. If larger aircraft rotates prior to the intersection, avoid flight below the larger aircraft's flightpath. Abandon the approach unless a landing is ensured well before reaching the intersection.

f. *Departing behind a large aircraft:* Note the larger aircraft's rotation point and rotate prior to the larger aircraft's rotation point. Continue climbing above the larger aircraft's climb path until turning clear of the larger aircraft's wake. Avoid subsequent headings that will cross below and behind a larger aircraft.

g. *Intersection takeoffs, same runway:* Be alert to adjacent larger aircraft operations, especially of your runway. If intersection takeoff clearance is received, avoid subsequent heading which will cross below a larger aircraft's path.

h. *Departing or landing after a larger aircraft executing a low approach, missed approach or touch-and-go landing:* Vortices settle and move laterally near the ground. Because of this, the vortex hazard may exist along the runway and in your flight path after a larger aircraft has executed a low approach, missed approach or a touch-and-go landing, particularly in light quartering wind conditions. You should ensure that an interval of at least 2 minutes has elapsed before your takeoff or landing.

i. *En route VFR (thousand-foot altitude plus 500 feet):* Avoid flight below and behind a large aircraft's path. If a larger aircraft is observed above or on the same track (meeting or overtaking) adjust your position laterally, preferably upwind.

Remember: Acceptance of instructions from ATC is an acknowledgment that the pilot will ensure safe takeoff and landing intervals and accept the responsibility for providing wake turbulence separation.

31. What are several examples of illusions that may lead to landing errors? (AIM 8-1-5)

Runway width illusion—A narrower-than-usual runway can create the illusion that the aircraft is at a higher altitude than it actually is. The pilot who does not recognize this illusion will fly a lower approach, with the risk of striking objects along the approach path or landing short. A wider-than-usual runway can have the opposite effect, with the risk of leveling out high and landing hard or overshooting the runway.

Runway and terrain slopes illusion—An upsloping runway, upsloping terrain, or both, can create the illusion that the aircraft is at a higher altitude than it actually is. The pilot who does not recognize this illusion will fly a lower approach. A downsloping runway, downsloping approach terrain, or both, can have the opposite effect.

Featureless terrain illusion—An absence of ground features, as when landing over water, darkened areas, and terrain made featureless by snow, can create the illusion that the aircraft is at a higher altitude than it actually is. The pilot who does not recognize this illusion will fly a lower approach.

Atmospheric illusions—Rain on the windscreen can create the illusion of greater height, and atmospheric haze can create the illusion of being at a greater distance from the runway. The pilot who does not recognize these illusions will fly a lower approach.

32. The acronym "LAHSO" refers to what specific air traffic control procedure? (AIM 4-3-11)

LAHSO is an acronym for "land and hold short operations." At controlled airports, ATC may clear a pilot to land and hold short of an intersecting runway, an intersecting taxiway, or some other designated point on a runway. Pilots may accept such a clearance provided that the pilot-in-command determines the aircraft can safely land and stop within the available landing distance (ALD). Student pilots or pilots not familiar with LAHSO should not participate in the program. Pilots are expected to decline a LAHSO clearance if they determine it will compromise safety or if weather is below basic VFR conditions (a minimum ceiling of 1,000 feet and 3 SM visibility).

33. Where can available landing distance (ALD) data be found? (AIM 4-3-11)

ALD data are published in the special notices section of the A/FD and in the U.S. Terminal Procedures Publications. Controllers will also provide ALD data upon request.

34. Where are runway incursions most likely to occur? (FSAT 00-09)

The runway incursions that are most likely to cause accidents generally occur at complex, high-volume airports such as those with parallel/intersecting runways, multiple taxiway/runway intersections, complex taxi patterns, and the need for traffic to cross active runways. Historical data also shows that a disproportionately large number of runway incursions involve general aviation pilots and often result from misunderstood controller instructions, confusion, disorientation, and/or inattention. Nearly all runway incursions are caused by human error.

35. What are several recommended practices concerning prevention of runway incursions? (FSAT 00-09)

a. Read back all runway crossing and/or hold short instructions.

b. Review airport layouts as part of preflight planning and before descending to land, and while taxiing as needed.

c. Know airport signage.

d. Review NOTAMs for information on runway/taxiway closures and construction areas.

e. Do not hesitate to request progressive taxi instructions from ATC when unsure of the taxi route.

f. Check for traffic before crossing any runway or entering a taxiway.

g. Turn on aircraft lights and rotating beacon or strobe lights while taxing.

h. When landing, clear the active runway as quickly as possible then wait for taxi instructions before further movement.

i. Study and use proper radio phraseology as describe in the AIM in order to respond to and understand ground control instructions.

j. Write down complex taxi instructions at unfamiliar airports.

36. Discuss recommended collision avoidance procedures and considerations in the following situations. (FAA-H-8083-25)

a. *Before takeoff*—Prior to taxiing onto a runway or landing area in preparation for takeoff, pilots should scan the approach area for possible landing traffic, executing appropriate maneuvers to provide a clear view of the approach areas.

b. *Climbs and descents*—During climbs and descents in flight conditions that permit visual detection of other traffic, pilots should execute gentle banks left and right at a frequency that allows continuous visual scanning of the airspace.

c. *Straight and level*—During sustained periods of straight-and-level flight, a pilot should execute appropriate clearing procedures at periodic intervals.

Continued

d. *Traffic patterns* — Entries into traffic patterns while descending should be avoided.

e. *Traffic at VOR sites* — Due to converging traffic, sustained vigilance should be maintained in the vicinity of VORs and intersections.

f. *Training operations* — Vigilance should be maintained and clearing turns should be made prior to a practice maneuver. During instruction, the pilot should be asked to verbalize the clearing procedures (call out clear "left, right, above, and below"). High-wing and low-wing aircraft have their respective blind spots. High-wing aircraft should momentarily raise the wing in the direction of the intended turn and look for traffic prior to commencing the turn. Low-wing aircraft should momentarily lower the wing.

Additional Study Questions

1. **Prior to departure, what items should you brief your passengers on?** (FAA-H-8083-3)

2. **When navigating by VOR, when will you have "reverse sensing?"** (FAA-H-8083-3)

3. **If your Mode C transponder fails while en route, can you continue flight into Class B or Class C airspace?** (AIM 4-1-19)

4. **While en route, how can a pilot determine the appropriate controlling agency to contact for information concerning flight operations into the following types of airspace: Restricted Area, Warning Area, Alert Area, Military Operations Area?** (AIM 3-4-1 through 3-4-6)

5. **Where can a pilot find information on the location of the nearest VOT testing station?** (AIM 1-1-4)

6. **Discuss the various factors a pilot should consider when making a Go/No-Go decision for a particular flight.**

7. How will you position your aircraft's flight control surfaces while taxiing in the following conditions: quartering tailwind, quartering headwind? (FAA-H-8083-3)

8. Demonstrate the following hand signals utilized by a lineman when directing you to or from a ramp: (AIM 4-3-25)

   a. All clear (OK)

   b. Start engine

   c. Pull chocks

   d. Come ahead

   e. Left turn

   f.   Right turn

   g. Slow down

   h. Stop

   i.   Insert chocks

   j.   Cut engines

   k. Emergency stop

9. What two factors should be considered when evaluating the type of survival equipment to carry for a flight over uninhabited terrain? (AIM 6-2-7)

10. Why is a postflight inspection recommended, and what are you looking for during that inspection? (FAA-H-8083-3)

Night
Operations

A. Night Preparation

1. Name the two distinct types of light-sensitive cells located in the retina of the eye. (FAA-H-8083-3)

Rods and cones are the light-sensitive cells located in the retina.

2. What is the function of the cones, and where are they located in the eye? (FAA-H-8083-3)

The cones are used to detect color, detail and far-away objects and are located in the center of the retina at the back of the eye. They are less sensitive to light, require higher levels of intensity to become active, and are most useful in the daylight hours.

3. What is the function of the rods, and where are they located in the eye? (FAA-H-8083-3)

Rods are located in the back of the eye or retina. The rods function when something is seen out of the corner of the eye or peripheral vision. They detect objects, particularly those that are moving, but do not give detail or color — only shades of gray. Both the cones and the rods are used for vision during daylight. In the absence of normal light, the process of night vision is placed almost entirely on the rods.

4. What is the average time it takes for the rods and cones to become adapted to darkness? (FAA-H-8083-3)

The cones will take approximately 10–15 minutes to adjust to darkness. The rods will take approximately 30 minutes to adjust to darkness.

5. What should the pilot do to accommodate changing light conditions? (FAA-H-8083-3)

The pilot should allow enough time for the eyes to become adapted to the low light levels, and then should avoid exposure to bright light which could cause temporary blindness.

6. Give several examples of illusions related to ground lighting conditions. (FAA-H-8083-3)

a. On a clear night, distant stationary lights can be mistaken for stars or other aircraft. Certain geometrical patterns of ground lights, such as a freeway, runway, approach, or even lights on a moving train can cause confusion. Dark nights tend to eliminate reference to a visual horizon.

b. A black-hole approach occurs when the landing is made from over water or non-lighted terrain where the runway lights are the only source of light. Without peripheral visual cues to help, pilots will have trouble orientating themselves relative to Earth. The runway can seem out of position (downsloping or upsloping) and in the worse case, results in landing short of the runway.

c. Night landings can be complicated by the difficulty of judging distance and the possibility of confusing approach and runway lights. For example, when a double row of approach lights joins the boundary lights of the runway, there can be confusion where the approach lights terminate and runway lights begin. Under certain conditions, approach lights can make the aircraft seem higher in a turn to final, than when its wings are level.

7. When approaching a well-lit runway surrounded by a dark area with little or no features, what illusion should a pilot be alert for? (AIM 8-1-5)

Featureless terrain illusion—an absence of ground features, as when landing over water, darkened areas, and terrain made feature-less by snow, can create the illusion that the aircraft is at a higher altitude than it actually is. The pilot who does not recognize this illusion will fly a lower approach.

8. What should the pilot do to maintain good eyesight? (FAA-H-8083-3)

Good eyesight depends upon physical condition. Fatigue, colds, vitamin deficiency, alcohol, stimulants, smoking, or medication can seriously impair vision.

9. **What can the pilot do to improve the effectiveness of vision at night?** (FAA-H-8083-3)

   a. Adapt the eyes to darkness prior to flight and keep them adapted. About 30 minutes is needed to adjust after exposure to a bright light.

   b. If oxygen is available, use it during night flying. Significant deterioration in night vision can occur at cabin altitudes as low as 5,000 feet.

   c. Close one eye when exposed to bright light to help avoid the blinding effect.

   d. Do not wear sunglasses after sunset.

   e. Move the eyes more slowly than in daylight.

   f. Blink the eyes if they become blurred.

   g. Concentrate on seeing objects.

   h. Force the eyes to view off center.

   i. Maintain good physical condition.

   j. Avoid smoking, drinking, and using drugs that may be harmful.

10. **What equipment should the pilot have for night flight operations?** (FAA-H-8083-3)

    At least one reliable flashlight is recommended as standard equipment on all night flights. A D-cell size flashlight with a bulb switching mechanism that can be used to select white or red light is preferable. The white light is used while performing the preflight visual inspection, and the red light is used when performing cockpit operations. A spare set of batteries is also recommended.

11. **What other items should the pilot have on board for night flights?** (FAA-H-8083-3)

    Pilots should have appropriate navigational charts, including any charts adjacent to the intended route of flight on board for night flight. These charts should be mounted on a clipboard or mapboard to prevent being lost in the dark cockpit.

12. Explain the arrangement and interpretation of the position lights on an aircraft. (FAA-H-8083-3)

A red light is located on the left wing tip, a green light is located on the right wing tip and a white light is located on the tail. If the pilot observes both a green and red light on another aircraft, then the other aircraft is generally approaching the pilot's position. If the pilot sees only a green light, then the other aircraft is moving left to right in relation to the pilot's position. If the pilot sees only a red light, then the aircraft is moving right to left in relation to the pilot's position.

13. Position lights are required to be on during what period of time? (14 CFR 91.209)

From sunset to sunrise.

14. When an aircraft is operated in, or in close proximity to, a night operations area, what is required of an aircraft? (14 CFR 91.209)

The aircraft must:

a. be clearly illuminated,

b. have position lights, or

c. be in an area which is marked by obstruction lights.

15. Are aircraft anticollision lights required to be on during night flight operations? (14 CFR 91.209)

Yes; however, the anticollision lights need not be lighted when the pilot-in-command determines that, because of operating conditions, it would be in the interest of safety to turn the lights off.

16. What are Runway End Identifier Lights (REIL)? (AIM 2-1-3)

REILs are installed at many airfields to provide rapid and positive identification of the approach end of a particular runway. The system consists of a pair of synchronized flashing lights located laterally on each side of the runway threshold. REILs may be omnidirectional or unidirectional facing the approach area.

17. Describe a Runway Edge Light System. (AIM 2-1-4)

Runway edge lights are used to outline the edges of runways during periods of darkness or restricted visibility conditions. They are white, except on instrument runways yellow replaces white on the last 2,000 feet or half the runway length, whichever is less, to form a caution zone for landings. The lights marking the ends of the runway emit red light toward the runway to indicate the end of runway to a departing aircraft and emit green outward from the runway end to indicate the threshold to landing aircraft. These light systems are classified according to the intensity or brightness they are capable of producing. Examples are: High Intensity Runway Lights (HIRL), Medium Intensity Runway Lights (MIRL), and the Low Intensity Runway Lights (LIRL).

18. Describe a Runway Centerline Lighting System (RCLS). (AIM 2-1-5)

Runway centerline lights—installed on some precision approach runways to facilitate landing under adverse visibility conditions. They are located along the runway centerline and are spaced at 50-foot intervals. When viewed from the landing threshold, the runway centerline lights are white until the last 3,000 feet of the runway. The white lights begin to alternate with red for the next 2,000 feet, and for the last 1,000 feet of the runway, all centerline lights are red.

19. What are Touchdown Zone Lights (TDZL)? (AIM 2-1-5)

Touchdown zone lights consist of two rows of transverse light bars disposed symmetrically about the runway centerline. The system consists of steady-burning white lights which start at 100 feet beyond the landing threshold and extend to 3,000 feet beyond the landing threshold or to the midpoint of the runway, whichever is less.

20. Describe several different types of taxiway lighting. (AIM 2-1-9)

a. *Taxiway edge lights*—outline the edges of taxiways; consist of blue lights.

b. *Taxiway centerline lights*—assists ground traffic in low visibility conditions; consists of steady-burning green lights.

c. *Clearance bar lights*—installed at holding positions on taxiways; consist of three in-pavement steady-burning yellow lights.

d. *Runway guard lights*—installed at taxiway/runway intersections; consists of either a pair of elevated flashing lights on either side of taxiway or in-pavement yellow lights installed across the taxiway.

e. *Stop bar lights*—used to confirm ATC clearance to enter or cross an active runway in low visibility conditions; consists of a row of red, unidirectional, steady-burning in-pavement lights installed across the taxiway and a pair of elevated steady burning red lights on each side.

21. What are the different types of rotating beacons used to identify airports? (AIM 2-1-8)

a. White and green .... Lighted land airport

b. *Green alone .... Lighted land airport

c. White & yellow .... Lighted water airport

d. *Yellow alone .... Lighted water airport

e. Green, yellow & white ....Lighted heliport

f. White (dual peaked & green) ....Lighted military airport

*Green alone or yellow alone is used only in connection with a white and green or white and yellow beacon display respectively.

22. Describe several types of obstruction lighting.
(AIM 2-2-3)

a. *Aviation red obstruction lights*—flashing aviation red beacons and steady burning aviation red lights during nighttime operations.

b. *Medium and high intensity white obstruction lights*—may be used during daytime and twilight with reduced intensity for nighttime operation. Not normally installed on structures less than 200 feet.

c. *Dual lighting*—a combination of flashing aviation red beacons and steady-burning aviation red lights for nighttime operations and flashing high intensity white lights for daytime operation.

d. *Catenary lighting*—medium and high intensity flashing white markers for high voltage transmission lines and support structures.

23. How does a pilot determine the status of a light system at a particular airport? (FAA-H-8083-3)

The pilot needs to check the Airport/Facility Directory and any Notices to Airmen (NOTAMs) to find out about available lighting systems, light intensities and radio-controlled light system frequencies.

24. How does a pilot activate a radio-controlled runway light system while airborne? (AIM 2-1-7)

The pilot activates radio-controlled lights by keying the microphone on a specified frequency. The following sequence can be used for typical radio controlled lighting systems:

a. On initial arrival, key the microphone seven times to turn the lights on and achieve maximum brightness.

b. If the runway lights are already on upon arrival repeat the above sequence to ensure a full 15 minutes of lighting.

c. The intensity of the lights can be adjusted by keying the microphone five or three times within 5 seconds.

B. Night Flight

1. During preflight what things should be done to adequately prepare for the night flight? (FAA-H-8083-3)

a. Study all weather reports and forecasts. Particular attention should be directed towards temperature/dewpoint spreads to detect the possibility of fog formation.

b. Calculate wind directions and speeds along the proposed route of flight to ensure accurate drift calculations, as night visual perception of drift is generally inaccurate.

c. Obtain applicable aeronautical charts for both the proposed route as well as adjacent charts, and mark lighted check-points clearly.

d. Review all radio navigational aids for correct frequencies and availability.

e. Check all personal equipment such as flashlights and portable transceivers for proper operation.

f. The aircraft should be thoroughly preflighted.

g. All aircraft position lights, as well as the landing light and rotating beacon, should be checked for proper operation.

h. Ground areas should be checked for obstructions that may not be readily visible from within the cockpit.

2. What are some guidelines to follow during the starting, taxiing, and run-up phases of a night flight? (FAA-H-8083-3)

a. The pilot should exercise extra caution on "clearing" the propeller arc area. The use of lights prior to and after engine start-up can also alert persons in the area to the presence of the active aircraft.

b. During taxiing, avoid unnecessary use of electrical equipment which would put an abnormal load on the electrical system, such as the landing light. Additionally, other pilots taxiing in the area can be blinded by your landing light or strobes, so avoid using them during taxiing.

c. Taxi slowly and follow any taxi lines.

3. **What are some of the guidelines to follow during takeoff and departure phases of a night flight?** (FAA-H-8083-3)

   a. During takeoff the pilot should:

   - on the initial takeoff roll, use both the distant runway edge lights as well as the landing light area to keep the aircraft straight and parallel in the runway, and

   - upon liftoff, keep a positive climb by referencing the attitude indicator along with positive rate of climb on the vertical speed indicator.

   b. During climbout:

   - do not initiate any turns until reaching safe maneuvering altitude, and

   - turn the landing light off after climb.

4. **What should the pilot do to provide proper orientation and navigation during a night flight?** (FAA-H-8083-3)

   a. Exercise caution to avoid flying into clouds or a layer of fog. Usually, the first indication of flying into restricted visibility conditions is the gradual disappearance of lights on the ground. If the lights begin to take on an appearance of being surrounded by a halo or glow, use caution in attempting further flight in that same direction, as this is indicative of ground fog.

   b. Practice and acquire competency in straight-and-level flight, climbs and descents, level turns, climbing and descending turns, and steep turns. Recovery from unusual attitudes should also be practiced, but only on dual flights with a flight instructor.

   c. Practice the above maneuvers with all the cockpit lights turned OFF—this type of "blackout" training will prove helpful later on, in the event of an electrical or instrument light failure. Include the use of the navigation equipment and local NAVAIDs in this exercise.

   d. Continually monitor position, time estimates, and fuel consumed. NAVAIDs, if available, should be used to assist in monitoring enroute progress.

5. If an engine failure occurs at night, what procedures should be followed? (FAA-H-8083-3)

If the engine fails at night, the same procedures apply for dealing with the situation in the daytime. Maintain positive control of the airplane—do not panic. A normal glide should be established and maintained and the airplane turned toward an airport or away from congested areas. A check should be made to determine the cause of the engine failure, such as position of the magnetos, fuel selectors, or primer. If unsuccessful in restart procedures, select 7700 on the transponder and 121.5 on your radio. Declare an emergency, stating WHO you are, WHERE you are, and WHAT your intentions are. In some cases, where radar is available (Approach Control, Center, etc.) you may obtain a quick vector to the nearest airport if within gliding distance. If you have done your homework, you planned your route of flight within gliding distance of lighted airports. If not, two possibilities exist for emergency landing areas:

Lighted areas—interstate highways, roads, parking lots, etc. Advantages include being able to see where and what you are landing on, and having a relatively improved surface to land upon. Disadvantages include all kinds of obstructions to deal with, such as wires, poles, traffic, etc.

Unlighted areas—dark areas with relatively few lights indicating an open area such as a field, lake, etc. Advantages include few or no obstructions to deal with. Disadvantages include not being able to see what you have selected to land on until illumination by your landing light, and the higher possibility that what you have selected is unimproved, rough terrain, etc. As nearly as possible, land into the wind, with flaps, at minimum approach speed. Complete a pre-landing checklist, and immediately before touchdown, secure all systems (electrical, fuel) and open the doors.

Whatever your decision, maintain positive control of the aircraft all the way down. A controlled crash will always be more survivable than an uncontrolled crash.

6. **What procedures should be followed during the approach and landing phase of a night flight?** (FAA-H-8083-3)

   a. The pilot should identify the airport and associated airport lighting and runway lighting.

   b. The aircraft should be flown towards the airport beacon until the runway lights are identified.

   c. A powered approach should be used because visual perception during a descent at night can be difficult.

   d. The landing light should be switched on upon entering the airport traffic area.

   e. The pilot should avoid the use of excessive speed on approach and landing.

Additional Study Questions

1. **What is good operating practice concerning the use of aircraft lighting (taxi, landing, strobes) while on the ground at night?** (FAA-H-8083-3)

2. **Why is it especially important to maintain an organized cockpit when flying at night?** (FAA-H-8083-3)

3. **When conducting an airplane preflight inspection for a local night flight, in addition to those involved in all flights, what are some general items that you should include?** (FAA-H-8083-3)

4. **What type of lighting indicates a displaced threshold?** (AIM 2-1-4)

5. **Discuss the various types of cockpit and exterior lighting equipment installed in your airplane.** (FAA-H-8083-3)

6. **What procedure should be utilized when attempting to land at night without a landing light?** (FAA-H-8083-3)

7. Why is it especially important pilots be current in basic attitude instrument flying procedures when flying at night? (FAA-H-8083-3)

8. During the enroute segment of a night flight, how can a pilot determine they are flying from VFR conditions to potentially marginal VFR or IFR conditions? (FAA-H-8083-3)

9. When planning a night flight (local or X/C), what weather information should be particularly significant to the pilot? (FAA-H-8083-3)

10. Discuss your method of route and checkpoint selection, when planning a night VFR cross-country flight. (FAA-H-8083-3)

Aeromedical
Factors

7

Flight Physiology

1. What is hypoxia? (AIM 8-1-2)

Hypoxia is a state of oxygen deficiency in the body sufficient to impair functions of the brain and other organs.

2. Where does hypoxia usually occur, and what symptoms should one expect? (AIM 8-1-2)

Although a deterioration in night vision occurs at a cabin pressure altitude as low as 5,000 feet, other significant effects of altitude hypoxia usually do not occur in the normal healthy pilot below 12,000 feet. From 12,000 feet to 15,000 feet of altitude, judgment, memory, alertness, coordination, and ability to make calculations are impaired, and headache, drowsiness, dizziness and either a sense of well-being or belligerence occur. Effects are worse above 15,000 feet.

3. What factors can make a pilot more susceptible to hypoxia? (AIM 8-1-2)

The altitude at which significant effects of hypoxia occur can be lowered by a number of factors. Carbon monoxide inhaled in smoking or from exhaust fumes, lowered hemoglobin (anemia), and certain medications can reduce the oxygen-carrying capacity of the blood. Small amounts of alcohol and low doses of certain drugs, such as antihistamines, tranquilizers, sedatives, and analgesics can, through their depressant action, render the brain much more susceptible to hypoxia. Extreme heat and cold, fever, and anxiety increase the body's demand for oxygen, and hence its susceptibility to hypoxia.

4. How can hypoxia be avoided? (AIM 8-1-2)

Hypoxia is prevented by heeding factors that reduce tolerance to altitude, by enriching the inspired air with oxygen from an appropriate oxygen system, and by maintaining a comfortable, safe cabin pressure altitude. For optimum protection, pilots are encouraged to use supplemental oxygen above 10,000 feet during the day, and above 5,000 feet at night.

5. What is hyperventilation? (AIM 8-1-3)

Hyperventilation, or an abnormal increase in the volume of air breathed in and out of the lungs, can occur subconsciously when a stressful situation is encountered in flight. This results in a significant decrease in the carbon dioxide content of the blood. Carbon dioxide is needed to automatically regulate the breathing process.

6. What symptoms can a pilot expect from hyperventilation? (AIM 8-1-3)

As hyperventilation "blows off" excessive carbon dioxide from the body, a pilot can experience symptoms of light-headedness, suffocation, drowsiness, tingling in the extremities, and coolness, and react to them with even greater hyperventilation. Incapacitation can eventually result from uncoordination, disorientation, and painful muscle spasms. Finally, unconsciousness can occur.

7. How can a hyperventilating condition be reversed? (AIM 8-1-3)

The symptoms of hyperventilation subside within a few minutes after the rate and depth of breathing are consciously brought back to normal. The buildup of carbon dioxide in the body can be hastened by controlled breathing in and out of a paper bag held over the nose and mouth.

8. What is carbon monoxide poisoning? (AIM 8-1-4)

Carbon monoxide is a colorless, odorless and tasteless gas contained in exhaust fumes. When inhaled, even in minute quantities over a period of time, it can significantly reduce the ability of the blood to carry oxygen. Consequently, effects of hypoxia occur.

9. How does carbon monoxide poisoning occur, and what symptoms should a pilot be alert for? (AIM 8-1-4)

Most heaters in light aircraft work by air flowing over the manifold. The use of these heaters while exhaust fumes are escaping through manifold cracks and seals is responsible every year for several nonfatal and fatal aircraft accidents from carbon monoxide poisoning. A pilot who detects the odor of exhaust or experiences symptoms of headache, drowsiness, or dizziness while using the heater should suspect carbon monoxide poisoning.

10. What action should be taken if a pilot suspects carbon monoxide poisoning? (AIM 8-1-4)

A pilot who suspects this condition to exist should immediately shut off the heater and open all air vents. If symptoms are severe, or continue after landing, medical treatment should be sought.

11. What is the cause of motion sickness, and what are its symptoms? (FAA-H-8083-25)

Motion sickness is caused by continued stimulation of the inner ear which controls the sense of balance. The symptoms are progressive. Pilots may experience loss of appetite, saliva collecting in the mouth, perspiration, nausea, and possible disorientation. The head aches and there may be a tendency to vomit. If allowed to become severe enough, the pilot may become incapacitated.

12. What action should be taken if a pilot or his passenger suffers from motion sickness? (FAA-H-8083-25)

If suffering from airsickness while piloting an aircraft, open up the air vents, loosen the clothing, use supplemental oxygen, and keep the eyes on a point outside the airplane. Avoid unnecessary head movements. Terminate the flight and land as soon as possible.

13. What is "ear block"? (AIM 8-1-2)

As the aircraft cabin pressure decreases during ascent, the expanding air in the middle ear pushes the Eustachian tube open. The air then escapes down to the nasal passages and equalizes in pressure with the cabin pressure. But during descent, the pilot must periodically open the Eustachian tube to equalize pressure. Either an upper respiratory infection, such as a cold or sore throat, or a nasal allergic condition can produce enough congestion around the Eustachian tube to make equalization difficult. Consequently, the difference in pressure between the middle ear and aircraft cabin can build to a level that will hold the Eustachian tube closed, making equalization difficult if not impossible. An ear block produces severe pain and loss of hearing that can last from several hours to several days.

14. What action can be taken to prevent ear block from occurring in flight? (AIM 8-1-2)

Normally this can be accomplished by swallowing, yawning, tensing muscles in the throat or, if these do not work, by the combination of closing the mouth, pinching the nose closed and attempting to blow through the nostrils (Valsalva maneuver). It is also prevented by not flying with an upper respiratory infection or nasal allergic condition.

15. What regulations apply and what common sense should prevail concerning the use of alcohol? (14 CFR 91.17)

The regulations prohibit pilots from performing crewmember duties within 8 hours after drinking any alcoholic beverage, while under the influence of alcohol, or having .04 percent weight or more alcohol in the blood. Due to the slow destruction of alcohol in the bloodstream, a pilot may still be under influence, or over the .04 percent mark, 8 hours after drinking a moderate amount of alcohol. Therefore, an excellent rule is to allow at least 12 to 24 hours from "bottle to throttle," depending on the amount of alcoholic beverage consumed.

16. What regulations apply and what common sense should prevail concerning the use of drugs and medication? (AIM 8-1-1)

Pilot performance can be seriously degraded by both prescribed and over-the-counter medications, as well as by the medical conditions for which they are taken. The regulations prohibit pilots from performing crewmember duties while using any medication that affects the faculties in any way contrary to safety. The safest rule is not to fly as a crewmember while taking any medication, unless approved to do so by the FAA.

17. Discuss the effects of nitrogen excesses during scuba diving upon a pilot or passenger in flight. (AIM 8-1-2)

A pilot or passenger who intends to fly after scuba diving should allow the body sufficient time to rid itself of excess nitrogen absorbed during diving. If not, decompression sickness due to evolved gas can occur during exposure to low altitude and create a serious inflight emergency. The recommended waiting times before flight are as follows:

Flight altitudes up to 8,000 feet:

- Wait at least 12 hours after diving which has not required a controlled ascent.
- Wait at least 24 hours after diving which has required controlled ascent.

Flight altitudes above 8,000 feet:

- Wait at least 24 hours after any scuba dive.

Note: The recommended altitudes are actual flight altitudes above mean sea level and not pressurized cabin altitudes. This takes into consideration the risk of decompression of the aircraft during flight.

Continued

Additional Study Questions

1. What are several factors which may contribute to impairment of a pilot's performance? (AIM 8-1-1)

2. What is spatial disorientation? (AIM 8-1-5)

3. Give several examples of illusions leading to spatial disorientation. (AIM 8-1-5)

4. How can you avoid spatial disorientation? (AIM 8-1-5)

5. What are symptoms of decompression sickness? (AIM 8-1-2)

6. When should a pilot be particularly alert for the possibility of carbon monoxide poisoning? (AIM 8-1-4)

7. What is sinus block? (AIM 8-1-2)

8. What are symptoms of sinus block? (AIM 8-1-2)

9. How can sinus block be prevented? (AIM 8-1-2)

10. Do regulations prohibit a pilot (with a current medical certificate) from flying if he/she has a known medical condition that occurs after medical certification? (14 CFR Part 67)

ADM and CRM   **8**

A. Aeronautical Decision Making

1. Define aeronautical decision making. (FAA-H-8083-9)

ADM is the systematic approach to the mental process used by aircraft pilots to consistently determine the best course of action in response to a given set of circumstances.

2. During flight, decisions must be made regarding events that involve interactions between the four risk elements. What are they? (FAA-H-8083-9)

Pilot-in-command – the aircraft – the environment – the operation

3. Which are the major factors affecting judgment and decision making? (FAA-H-8083-9)

Stress – health – attitude – experience

4. Name the five hazardous attitudes that negatively impact a pilot's judgment and ability to make competent decisions and their antidotes. (FAA-H-8083-9)

Attitudes	Antidotes
Anti-authority	Follow the rules, they are usually right.
Impulsivity	Think first — not so fast.
Invulnerability	It could happen to me.
Macho	Taking chances is foolish.
Resignation	I can make a difference, I am not helpless.

B. Crew Resource Management

1. What does crew resource management (CRM) refer to? (FAA-H-8083-9)

CRM is the application of team management concepts in the flight deck environment. It was initially known as "cockpit resource management," but as CRM programs evolved to include cabin crews, maintenance personnel, and others, it became "crew resource management." This includes single pilots, since pilots of small aircraft, as well as crews of larger aircraft, must make effective use of all available resources—human resources, hardware, and information.

2. Discuss the importance of understanding the concept of positive exchange of flight controls, as it relates to flight training. (FAA-H-8083-9)

During flight training, there must always be a clear understanding between students and flight instructors of who has control of the aircraft. Prior to flight, a briefing should be conducted that includes the procedure for the exchange of flight controls. A positive three-step process in the exchange of flight controls between pilots is a proven procedure and one that is strongly recommended.

3. Describe the three-step process used for the positive exchange of flight controls. (FAA-H-8083-9)

During this procedure, a visual check is recommended to see that the other person actually has the flight controls. When returning the controls to the instructor, the student should follow the same procedure the instructor used when giving control to the student. The student should stay on the controls and keep flying the aircraft until the instructor says, "I have the flight controls." There should never be any doubt as to who is flying the aircraft.

- When the flight instructor wishes the student to take control of the aircraft, the instructor says to the student: *"You have the flight controls."*
- The student acknowledges immediately by saying: *"I have the flight controls."*
- The flight instructor again says: *"You have the flight controls."*

C. Use of Checklists

1. Why are pilots encouraged to use checklists?
(FAA-H-8083-3)

Checklists provide a logical and standardized method to operate a particular make and model airplane. Following a checklist reinforces the use of proper procedures throughout all major phases of flight operations.

2. What are the two primary methods for using checklists?
(FAA-H-8083-3)

a. *Read and Do*—This is when the pilot picks up a checklist, refers to an item, and sets the condition. The items for any particular phase of flight would all be accomplished before the checklist is set aside.

b. *Do and Verify*—Set the condition of the items for a particular phase of operation from memory or flow pattern, then use the checklist and read to verify that the appropriate condition for each item in that phase has been set. It is not wise for a pilot to become so reliant upon a flow pattern that he or she fails to verify with a checklist. Checking important items solely from memory is not an acceptable substitute for checklists.

Additional Study Questions

1. **The DECIDE model for decision making involves which elements?** (FAA-H-8083-9)

2. **What criteria may be used by a pilot when evaluating flying risks?** (FAA-H-8083-9)

3. **Describe the three stressors representing a barrier to effective decision making.** (FAA-H-8083-9)

4. **Most of the hazards in flying can be minimized by adopting what general philosophy?** (FAA-H-8083-9)

5. **Which groups routinely working with the cockpit crew may also be viewed as effective components of CRM and the decision making process in the cockpit?** (FAA-H-8083-9)

Maneuvers Table

Appendix 1

1 **Appendix**

Private Pilot Practical Test Standards (condensed)

Task	Objective Minimum acceptable standard of performance			
Takeoff Normal/Crosswind Short/Soft	V_Y +10 / -5 V_X +10 / -5, then V_Y +10 / -5			
Landing Normal/Crosswind Forward Slip Short Soft Go Around	1.3 V_{SO} +10 / -5, touch at or within 400 feet beyond target Min float, touch at or within 400 feet beyond target 1.3 V_{SO} +10 / -5, touch at or within 200 feet beyond target 1.3 V_{SO} +10 / -5, touch at minimum speed and descent rate Power (Carb Heat off?), pitch for V_Y +10 / -5, flaps, gear			
Emergency Operations Emergency Approach and Landing	Use recommended descent configuration and airspeed ±10 kts.			
		Heading or bank ±°	**Altitude ±ft**	**Speed ±kts**
Traffic Pattern	Accurate track and safe spacing		100	10
Pilotage/NAV/Diverting	Know position ±3 NM	15	200	ETA ±5min

Instrument Flying
 Straight and level
 Constant airspeed climb and
  descend
 Turns and rollouts on heading
 Communications, Navigation,
  Radar Services
 Recovery from unusual attitudes
	
	Recover to stabilized
	flight w/o excesses
		20
		20
		
		10
		20
			200
			200
			
			200
			200
				10
				10
				
				10
				10

Slow Flight and Stalls (no flight
 below 1,500 AGL)
 Power-off Stalls
 	
Power-on Stalls
 	
Maneuvering during Slow Flight
  (straight & level, turns, climbs,
  descents)
	
	Straight & level or max.
	20° bank ±10°
	
	S±10° & L or max. 20°
	bank ±10°
		
		10
		
		10
		
		10
			
			100
				
				MCA +10/-0

Performance Maneuvers
 Steep turns
  360° with 45° ±5° bank,
  coordinated
		10	100	10

Ground Reference Maneuvers	Remain 600–1,000 AGL		100	10

1 Appendix

Applicant's Practical Test Checklist

Appendix 2

Applicant's Practical Test Checklist

Appointment with Examiner _____

Examiner's Name _____

Location _____

Date/Time _____

Acceptable Aircraft

Aircraft Documents

___ Airworthiness Certificate

___ Registration Certificate

___ Operating Limitations

Aircraft Maintenance Records

___ Logbook Record of Airworthiness Inspections and AD Compliance

___ Pilot's Operating Handbook, FAA-Approved Airplane Flight Manual

___ Current Weight and Balance Data

Personal Equipment

___ View-Limiting Device

___ Current Aeronautical Charts

___ Computer and Plotter

___ Flight Plan Form

___ Flight Logs

___ Current AIM, Airport Facility Directory, and Appropriate Publications

Personal Records

___ Identification — Photo/Signature ID

___ Pilot Certificate

___ Current and Appropriate Medical Certificate

___ Completed FAA Form 8710-1, Airman Certificate and/or Rating Application with Instructor's Signature (if applicable)

___ Computer Test Report

___ Pilot Logbook with Appropriate Instructor Endorsements

___ FAA Form 8060-5, Notice of Disapproval (if applicable)

___ Approved School Graduation Certificate (if applicable)

___ Examiner's Fee (if applicable)

Notes

Notes

Notes

Notes